THE BOOK ON SALES & MARKETING

EXPERT MARKETING FOR NON-MARKETERS

ASHLEY WILKES WEBBER

THE BOOK ON SALES AND MARKETING

COPYRIGHT © 2019 by Ashley Wilkes Webber

All rights reserved. No part of this book may be reproduced or used in any manner without written permission of the copyright owner except for the use of quotations in a book review.

First paperback edition, 2019

ISBN #: *9780578503790*

Library of Congress Control Number: *2019911221*

For Rush & Loki - Inherit the world

Table of Contents

1. ORIENTATION 1
2. YOU: The Journey 5
3. TARGET MARKETING 101 11
4. TARGET MARKETING 201 17
5. FUNNELS 101 25
6. TARGET MARKETING 301 33
7. SALES 101 39
8. SOCIAL MEDIA 101 47
9. NETWORKING 101 61
10. FUNNELS 201 71
11. CONTENT 101 93
12. CONTENT 201 99
13. SALES 201 113
14. SALES 301. 127
15. SALES 401 141
16. FUNNELS 301 155
17. CONTENT 301 167
18. WEB FUNDAMENTALS 179

19. NETWORKING 201	*193*
20. SOCIAL MEDIA 201	*201*
21. THE MEDIA	*219*
22. COMMENCEMENT	*229*
Vocabulary/Appendix	*233*
Notes	*256*

*Dedicated to my mother, Loma
Nam Myōhō Renge Kyō.*

CHAPTER 1

ORIENTATION

"Roads? Where we're going we don't need roads"
(Back to the Future, 1985)

What will it take for your business to claim its rightful place? A revolutionary new product? A tantalizing offer? The perfect branding? An amazing pitch? The answer is none of the above. Neither is inspiration, "hustle,"or "grind." **Not alone, anyway.**

It doesn't matter if you're a **"<u>solopreneur,</u>"** operate a storefront, or have employees numbering in the dozens; you'll need stronger processes guided by strategic *target marketing* if you intend on making your future results more successful than your past.

Welcome to *The Book on Sales and Marketing.*

The the most important sale you'll ever make is to yourself. If you can't believe wholeheartedly that what you have is worth someone else's money, they won't either.

Those with genuine enthusiasm for the value their company provides will always outperform someone just going through the motions. If you don't already, it's important to find a way to make yourself believe that what you are selling can change peoples lives for the better because it likely does whether it's obvious or not.

Sales and marketing are actually two very different disciplines working in tandem, both deeply rooted in the art of negotiation. Those set on success must be willing to challenge and persuade others when necessary. A resourceful marketer will earn the '*yes*' largely by building an immunity to the word 'no,' because they will hear it a lot. More valuable than having natural sales talent is a tolerance for practice and persistence.

Before we had money we traded things, and we're still largely operating on this kind of mentality. Your business and its customers aren't only transacting in dollars and cents, on a subconscious level you are actually dealing in perceived value. When someone perceives that the value they'll gain is worth more than the money they'll invest, they will act - whether or not there is proof that this is true. It's your responsibility to turn qualified prospects perceptions by overcoming their objections, settling their doubts, and encouraging them to invest in you as the solution.

Every business needs a **"Chief Marketing Officer (C.M.O.)"** or "*Chief Marketer*," in place to keep the value proposition clear and the message focused. If you are the owner or manager of a business and are currently shorthanded in that department, congratulations that person is you.

ORIENTATION

The role of the marketer is indispensable. Every operation, despite the quality of what it produces or its prestige, must display upfront to its audience that it has a product they want, backed by a company they trust, that can be purchased easily from someone they like, and that doesn't happen by accident.

As the C.M.O., the success or failure of your operation is squarely in your hands. It's not just a paycheck at stake: your team depends on you. Your partner depends on you. Your family and friends depend on you. Your children and their children depend on you. The people you serve depend on you.

Submitted for your consideration, this humble contribution is designed to help conserve precious time and resources on your journey to reach more of the people who need what you do. May it help you grow quickly so that you can get out there to build, spend, employ, influence and do what you do best… lead.

Time waits for no-one.

CHAPTER 2

YOU: THE JOURNEY

"Heroes get remembered but legends never die"
(The Sandlot, 1993)

Before diving into marketing strategies, funnels, lead generation, content creation, sales tools and other important mechanics, we're going to take a few minutes to talk about your responsibilities in this operation.

Your potency as Chief Marketer is directly linked to how well you can listen & communicate...

The *Chief Marketing Officer(C.M.O.)* must become completely in tune with the audience they are best suited for in the market, and that means careful research and observation. In order to best direct your businesses marketing resources and build profitable networks, you'll need to achieve complete clarity on exactly who you need to reach and what specifically makes you the best fit for them. It's the only way you'll be able to competently communicate, online or anywhere else.

When it comes to finding new leads, following up, creating visuals, writing copy, implementing different changing online platforms, generating content, maintaining different social media outlets, and everything else it takes to stay on top of your role as C.M.O., you may be tempted to think it's all in a days work, right?

Just because you are responsible for all of these things, certainly doesn't mean that you need to (or should) be doing them all yourself.

There are just too many different expertises out there in the modern marketplace for one person to master; it would be unreasonable to expect anyone to do it alone (even if that person is a rockstar *solopreneur*).

You don't always need to know the right answer, but you do need to know where to find it - quickly.

When it comes to scaling any sales model, the *C.M.O.* needs to align themselves with other entities who can help their operation grow. The partners, affiliates, and service providers you build relationships with can determine the resources and technology you can access and even its price point.

You need to realize that people aren't just buying a service or product from your business, they are buying part of a story. Your history. Your authority. These things have all become more and more intertwined as the influence of media has spread.

Believe it or not, marketing and cinema have quite a bit in common. The best movies aren't about movie stars, or special effects, or gimmicks: they are about people, the characters, and the human connection between them. They are about the **"journey."**

Your customers and potential customers want to get a better sense of who you are and what your company stands for, but more importantly they want to know "*why you?*"

Just like in any great movie, it's the journey that gives a regular person the right to be the hero, just as your journey gives you the right to serve your customers far better than anybody else in the market.

The big guys mess this up all the time. You are so much more than a logo and catchphrase.

Building a stronger foundation for your efforts is dramatically smoother with mastery of these fundamentals:

"The 5 Primary Elements of a Potent C.M.O.:"

1. *Consistency*: Product + Lead + Sales Process = Revenue. The Marketer knows that sales are the pulse of their business. Always follow up again.

2. *Connection*: the Marketer's network is their most powerful natural resource. *Who* you know is superior to *what* you know. Always be looking to expand the network.

3. *Innovation*: the Marketer who is adaptable and open to their next product, experience, trend, or upgrade will see around corners. Always be innovating.

4. *Vitality*: the Marketer who values their wellness

attracts others of high caliber, is charismatic, and persuasive. Preserve your body, mind, and spirit.

5. ***Philanthropy***: the Marketer that supports their community will earn their community's support. Always find ways to give back.

Developing in these areas will supercharge your effectiveness exponentially and it won't be long before you're gaining the traction you seek with more and more momentum, but Rome wasn't built in a day.

Resist the temptation to become overwhelmed on your journey when things get tough, because they will. Stay organized. Create a strategic plan based on what you're learning, implement changes brick by brick, and watch your influence expand.

This is the book on sales & marketing so there won't be a deep dive on executive development, but you should absolutely begin by taking a hard look at yourself as you are currently and participate in an honest personal inventory: which traits and skills are you naturally strong at? Which take the most effort? What will you need to fill the gaps?

Personal awareness of your assets and liabilities will make it so much easier to put the right solutions in place as they become available. It's not your job to be perfect but it is your job to be aware.

Use this guide not only for building a bigger, healthier and more robust business but most importantly becoming a stronger version of yourself as the Chief Marketing

Officer. The type who will thrive in not just this business but anything you touch.

When you commit to becoming more effective: connecting with the right people, becoming more visible in the community, following up consistently with every lead, and more - the world will reward you with more than just more revenue. You'll be better respected by your peers, envied by your competitors, and your loved ones will be proud of your accomplishments as if they were their own. You can influence the world; but it all begins with the right target...

CHAPTER 3

TARGET MARKETING 101:
The 80/20 rule

"Elementary, my dear Watson"
(The Adventures of Sherlock Holmes, 1939)

The *80/20 rule,* or *Pareto's Principal,* is deceptively simple but in turn, very effective. After discovering its considerable influence on so many successful people over the years, I tried implementing it myself and honestly I wish I'd found it sooner.

If you're someone who's really looking to get the most out of *target marketing* it's advantageous to understand the logic behind why it works - so that you aren't just following along. It's very possible that you're using the 80/20 rule in your own ways already, in which case this will serve as a reaffirmation in strategic focus; but no matter where you fall in the spectrum, *Pareto's Principle* can always help you get better results out of your marketing budgets, sales efforts, and daily productivity, all with no math required.

Two facts alone should influence the way you think about your business from here on:

1. 20% of your top products or services will generate 80% of your total sales,

2. 20% of your top customers generate 80% of your total revenue.

If this is new information for you it might be hard to believe, but it's a seemingly cosmic force that gets even weirder the deeper you dig:

- 20% of top beer drinkers make up 80% of all beer sales
- 20% of your clothing you wear 80% of the time
- 20% of your top distractions cause 80% of wasted time
- 20% of your activities take up 80% of your day
- 20% of actions accounts for 80% of productivity
- 20% of nations control just over 80% of the world's wealth… and that's only scratching the surface.

In the late 1800s, an Italian economist named Vilfredo Pareto published a study observing that 80% of Italian land was owned by just 20% of the population. "Hmmm."

Then he noticed that approximately 80% of the peas in his garden originated from just 20% of his highest producing pea plants. "Double hmmm."

I don't know what would make someone connect the two but since then mathematicians, economists, sociologists, and marketers have been spotting this phenomena everywhere, and I really mean everywhere. It would forever become known as **"Pareto's Principle"** or **"the 80/20 Rule:"**

"20% of top efforts yield 80% of total results"

Obviously we'll be implementing this concept specifically in your sales and marketing, but how exactly? It's simple: Invest more of your resources like time, money, and focus into the things that generate your primary results. Then find ways to remove or minimize all of the other distractions getting in the way.

Pareto's principle drastically improves the performance of your advertising dollars, offers, promotions, *reach*, and **"R.O.I."** (*Return on Investment*) overall, and that in itself is huge but there's much more:

Example: let's imagine you have a total of 500 customers generating $5000 in revenue. You might say you have a cumulative average of $10 per customer. But alone, that number would actually be misleading as it doesn't account for the behavior of special individuals within the group. For that you'll need Pareto's Principal to dig deeper.

The 80/20 Rule projects that around $4000 of business is actually coming from only 100 of your best customers, which also means,

- 20% of your 100 best customers (20) spend about ten times the average: $100 each.

- 20% of those 100 best customers (4) are spending twice as much as that again: $200 each.

- Your one, absolute best customer, likely spends twice as much again: $400.

These higher performing patrons are your business's **"loyal customers"** or **"loyals"** for short, and the top

20% among them are often known lovingly as *"whales."* But before you learn more about their influence in your business, ask yourself this: What would happen to your bottom line if you generated 10 more of these top performing loyal customers this month? Or 20? Or 100?

You'd probably agree that this top 20% of high-performers are considerably more valuable to you than other average customers - it's an objective fact. Obviously, everyone you serve is important, but since *loyal customers* will likely spend more per transaction, come back more frequently, and recommend you to their friends more often than most, it should be clear to see why you should take special care to nurture these relationships over time.

It's incredibly important to strategically provide the right incentives for *loyal customers* to stay engaged. These top producers and others like them are the magic behind growing faster. Within them is the DNA to your sales and marketing success overall but before you can extract the data you have to crack the code.

> **Fact**: A Harley loyal will find the money to buy a Harley regardless of income or situation. A Coca-Cola loyal will go across the street if the place they are in only carries Pepsi. A Disney loyal doesn't care about what big actor Dreamworks gets for their new animated film. Apple loyals don't care what features you pack into a smart phone - if it's not Apple you may as well go home... all because of the effectiveness of their targeting and how its position resonates with their base so well. They "click."
>
> **Do you have an engagement plan for your businesses current and future *loyal customers*?**

Businesses who focus their efforts on attracting and retaining more of these top 20% of *"loyal customers"* (and more like them) will spend less time trying to get in front of people who probably weren't as good of a fit in the first place. In turn, this shortens their **"sales cycle"** and reduces the cost and labor of converting leads into new customers.

This becomes even more useful later on when you start increasing your advertising budget to really get the *traffic* flowing. You'll already know how to be exactly in the right spot with the right message, saving yourself a ton of expensive trial and error.

Now, consider for a moment: if 80% of your revenue is coming from the top 20% of your best customers, then what is it specifically about this group of individuals that makes them behave the way they do? What ties them together? What do they have in common? **What are their patterns?**

Therin lies exactly how 80/20 will unlock better results for your business - but first you'll need to properly analyze the data.

By deciphering the specific characteristics that your top 20% of loyal customers share and then simply reverse-engineering the marketing for a person with these specific key traits to match, the traffic that responds are much more predisposed to behaving like your other best customers. Make sense?

That makes leads generated with *target marketing* worth exponentially more than the average customer who finds you off the street. You can even project their purchasing behaviors.

This is the foundation of modern **<u>target marketing</u>:** the art and science of appealing to someone with a specific set of ideal traits instead of just anyone who may need what you do.

With a clear vision of the top 20% of your customer base it becomes much easier to craft special messaging with precise imagery that pushes just the right buttons for attracting your qualified future *loyal customers*. These are the customers who are going to help you grow the fastest.

But which buttons are the right buttons?

CHAPTER 4

TARGET MARKETING 201:
The Hypothesis "Everybody = Nobody"

"If you don't know what you want, you end up with a lot you don't" (Fight Club, 1999)

> **FACT:** *When you are talking to everyone, you're really talking to no-one.*

It's estimated that the average American consumer is exposed to more than 4000 ads every single day and that number is on the rise. Billboards, television, radio, social media, news sites, pop-ups, bus benches and everywhere in between.

It probably doesn't also surprise you to find out that with so much bombarding a person every day, the target audience you are trying to connect with is experiencing sensory overload like never before, making it way much harder for them to receive your message - even if you are the perfect fit for them and can theoretically change their life.

This makes traditional **"broadcast marketing"** strategies very tricky for smaller businesses who are competing with huge companies in the open sea of advertising.

How do you cut through the clutter? How do you make sure that your potential *loyal customers* hear you loud and clear without the risk of destroying your budget competing with everyone else?

Case Study: During a **"deep dive"** a few years back, I found myself having an all too familiar conversation with a new client. We needed to make some initial decisions about the direction of their upcoming campaign and that included dialing in on their **"ideal customer"** or **"target customer"** for their media and sales content, but there was a huge problem...

Even though they'd been in business for several years and done relatively well in their space, the owner and her team had no idea who their target customer actually was. Worst of all, when pressed she insisted that she wanted to target "anyone who has experienced back pain," even going as far as to say she was looking for "anyone with a back."

Well, that makes things very difficult as that would literally include everyone on Earth and there's absolutely no way you can hone a message to fit everyone that doesn't just become more noise among all the other ads out there.

Everybody = Nobody

We pulled their revenue list from the past two years only to find that their biggest accounts actually had a few very important things in common:

- All of them came in to try acupuncture for the first time: We learned that it was easier to get people to try eastern medicine once than it was to get people to change from their current acupuncturist - if you liked it already, you probably have a provider you rely on.
- All of them were corporate: they all worked for big companies in the area with good insurance that covered their treatment in full at a higher rate - nothing out of pocket.
- They had families: Their top five accounts had a spouse and children that also came in for treatment under the same insurance; multiplying their dollar value of their account exponentially.

These people, this 20%, made up just under 80% of their revenue and my clients didn't even realize it.

Using just this data alone, it's clear that we aren't just looking for anyone who's had back pain and we're certainly not just looking for anyone who has a back. We are looking for corporate employees with back pain who have never had acupuncture before AND their families.

This is a specific person that you can search out and appeal to with a specific message. You know what language to use, what imagery to use (or not use). You know what their pain-points are. You know what's valuable to them. You know what they like. You can easily figure out where they spend their time. Once you know your real target, the game has changed simply because you're no longer operating blind.

You can become more than the thing that you do.

With an eye on your top 20% and the power it has over your bottom line, the next step is mapping out their identity on paper so we can start finding more people who are also prequalified to be high value or *loyal customer* material just like them. Only after completing your **"target map"** can we pinpoint exactly where to find your target without wasting precious time or money in the wrong places. You may ask yourself, how do I know these details? You fall into one of two categories:

- You are in business now, in which case you need to compile a list of current customers who've already paid you, break them down and see which ones have spent the most. Start the target mapping process from there.
- You aren't established yet, so the mapping process will require a certain amount of projection and guesswork on your part. Remember, your projections will help land you in the right general area but don't let your tentative map dictate your long term strategy unless you have some other hard data to back it up. At one point you will have collected concrete information; use it as soon as you can.

There are other people who do what you do. But there are things that are unique about you that make the leads you are looking for a better fit than those in the wider population you may be able to serve.

Are you on the high end or the low end? Are you premium or for a wider audience? Here are the fundamentals you need to get started on your *Target Map*:

Identify: This will include all the physical characteristics we can pick out about our target. What do they do for a living? CEO, Office middle management, or construction worker? How much do they make? $30K or 6-figures? Are they male or female? Your audiences will always skew one way or the other. How old? Teenage, college, 30-40, mature? Are they employed or stay at home? What are they driving? Car, truck, or SUV? How old is it? What brands do they prefer? What handbag or watch do they wear? Are they parents? How many kids do they have? How old are their kids? Do they have a college education? Are they single or in a relationship? Are they in a particular "stage" in their life? These are just some of things you will need to know about your buyer.

Qualify: Many people may need what you provide, but that doesn't make them your target necessarily. Qualifying a lead or target is all about identifying their behavior as it relates to the problem that you solve. Don't be afraid to be honest. You can't help someone if you aren't crystal clear on who they really are. Are they in a hurry? Some flower shops make a fortune in advertising last minute gifts and same day flowers. Their target procrastinates. Are they cheap? Walmart sells things at just above cost because they know they have a huge *target audience* that is on a tight budget. Costco's target has families with a higher income so they pass the savings on by operating in bulk, even though the overall average transaction is higher. This wouldn't work with Walmart's audience even though they sell many of the same products. Getting it? Are they ambitious? Take advantage of it like Nike, "Just do it." Do they care about appearances? Keep going.

Locate: Where do they spend their time offline? Do they go to yoga? Do they go to sports bars? Do they go to church? Do they go to clubs? Do they go to kid friendly places? Do they go to the dog park? Where do they live? Do they go to the home show or any other hobby events? Do they go to business conferences? If so, in what industries? Do they go to live events? If so, which ones? Where? Where do they get their news? Your city probably has a college and possibly a military base. Does your business serve people within these segments? How about their spouses? How about their parents? How about their kids?

Very often getting in front of someone is more practical than untrained marketers expect. If you know exactly who you are looking for it will always be easier to insure a return on your investment than if you don't. Use your target map to be in the right place at the right time with the right message.

You are looking for **"traffic:"** an active audience, rich with qualified potential customers.

So ask yourself, what does it cost to get a table topper at their local restaurant? A flier at their kids karate class? A wall-cling at their local gym? A *booth* at their networking event? Sponsoring lunch at their next corporate meeting? Their working space? Their women's group? Your cup runneth over. This is one of the places where you must begin to really exercise your resourcefulness. Be creative.

Next, consider where they spend their time online. What **"major medias"** like TV, radio, and newspaper do they consume? What social media do they frequent? What do they do for entertainment?

It's important to know that online advertisement is incredibly accessible and when done properly, cost efficient. You will be learning about ad buying in upcoming chapters, but for now, just know that a lot of the best moves you can make online are passive rather than active. People are already hanging out in groups, meaning all you have to do is tap in rather than start creating an audience from scratch, which is a great option, but a lot of work.

Be sure to thoroughly complete a *Target Map* before immediately jumping to the ad-buying stage, It will help you gain traction without spending near as much of your marketing budget directly on reach.

Even businesses operating exclusively or primarily online shouldn't skip the customer mapping process because it still influences their target's buying behaviors even when they aren't shopping in person.

It's important to know who you're looking for, but it's also just as important to know who you aren't. But what does that mean?

If someone in a suit walks into a Harley-Davidson showroom, they will happily sell him a motorcycle, but that's not their primary audience or who their ads are targeted at for a reason. They market to the seasoned biker in leather because that more closely represents their actual *loyal customer* base.

Obviously if someone wants to buy from you we aren't going to stop them, but for the sake of the sales and marketing strategy we need to know who is the best for us to make sure we aren't sinking resources into chasing leads that don't fit that target audience.

You may serve homeowners; chances are young single people aren't going to be your target so advertising around the local university may not be as good of an investment as seeking out face time with local homeowner associations;

that could yield exponentially better results.

Answer these questions correctly and you'll be ready to generate a cohesive marketing plan that will build a business capable of providing for generations. But before we talk about how to speak your target's language, we need to know what to do with all of this precious information as it's collected…

CHAPTER 5

FUNNELS 101:
Lists, Databases, & Tracking

"I'll be back" (The Terminator, 1984)

What is your "list?" Who and what exactly belongs on it? Where do you put it? What are you supposed to do with it once you have one? How does it actually make your business more money? All very common sources of confusion for people new to professional sales and marketing. Here are the facts:

It isn't always sexy but make no mistake, the dollars are definitely in the data. With a few easy steps you will be on your way to turning neglected business cards into real revenue. Surprisingly, 80% of businesses and the self-employed either don't have a functional list or are using theirs wrong. Which is a shame as it's one of the most versatile and effective marketing tools they've got.

A **"list"** or **"database"** is a lot more than just your digital Rolodex where professional contact info is kept, but conceptually that's a good place to start if this is new to you.

Some of the basics you will want to collect on your list include:

- Names
- Company names
- Phone numbers
- Email addresses
- Physical addresses
- Sales notes

But you will also want to begin to include things like:

- Order history
- Date met
- **"Lead source"**
- Social media info
- Birthday
- **"Sales stage"**

And anything else you can think of that will help you build a relationship with the contact. Depending on your industry, you will want to be on the lookout for different specific types of information to help your sales efforts be more proactive, these are **"data fields."** If you work with teams for big businesses you may want to document how many employees your contact has. If you help small businesses scale, you may want to document their annual revenue. A clothing store may want to keep gender or clothing size on hand. These extra pieces of information will help you maintain a more intimate relationship with your valuable contacts over time, so whenever you can collect more info, you absolutely should.

More information is always better - as long as it's generated ethically and kept safely in one place.

For many business owners and marketers there are four primary contact types they will need for a strong database: leads, customers, affiliates, and partners. Leads are potential opportunities, customers are anyone who has given you money whether that be a dollar or a million dollars, **"affiliates"** are people who have access to or influence over potential new leads, partners are anyone from service providers, vendors, and other people who help you run your business.

Best of all, when it's time to produce some fast revenue, you'll know exactly which targeted offer is for whom, because everyone will be kept neatly in this one place for easy access: on your list. But more than just a collection of contact information for convenience sake, your list is a physical representation of your influence in the market and in many ways the overall health of your businesses marketing as a whole.

If this is your very first database be aware that you don't need any special software to get started. Any free spreadsheet tool will do at the moment. If you're already using a software or **"C.R.M. (customer relationship manager)"** you're already on the right track and you'll find out how to develop it and make it stronger coming up. If you don't have a list at all, don't despair, here's the golden rule:

Whatever you do, don't wait to start building. Begin immediately - as soon as you finish this chapter even.

With a little direction I've seen entrepreneurs cobble together their very first profitable lists over an afternoon so there is no excuse for not having one. Also, be aware that **"Google Sheets"** is a reliable, (and free) easy **"spreadsheet"** application that allows you to begin a new project from the Google account you should already have in moments.

Other tools like Excel are great and if you kick it old school like that, please feel free to use them. The only guideline for list building is that it must be built within a spreadsheet that has the ability to generate a *"C.S.V. file"* with your information. *"C.S.V.,"* short for **"comma separated value,"** is a standardized file type that's easily shared between all of the major *Customer Relationship Management systems* or *C.R.M.s* and the other tools that become necessary as your business grows. This means no Word documents or text processors.

Be mindful when using a blank spreadsheet to collect lots of information that you'll have to create a column for each different piece of stored data resulting in a very long and potentially unruly database. But once you grow into a proper *C.R.M.* you can easily add tons of different types of info in the form of tags, notes, or custom fields which you will also be learning more about soon.

Beginning your first list can be as simple as opening a new spreadsheet and naming the columns. Name the first column, "First Name", the second column, "Last Name", the next, "Email", and then, "Phone Number", and so on with as many types of information as you feel will be valuable and you have access to. It's as easy as that.

First Name	Last Name	Email	Phone #	Etc...
Michael				
Jim				
Pam				
Dwight				

Next, go through every business email, text, Facebook message, order form, invoice, e-commerce platform, etc., and input everyone's information into the list as best you can.

After creating this workspace in the spreadsheet, I'd then hunt down every business card floating around The Office and take the time to enter it all in this one centralized place. Only then can you begin to weaponize and deploy your data with **<u>funnels.</u>**

I like to keep birthdates, date, and location where I met someone, company name, and lots of other things because that gives me power down the line to build a deeper relationship with them beyond just direct sales or marketing. Very much like the old days, *"I know you."*

You are strongly encouraged to do the same whenever possible.

It may be hard to accept, but building a list is non-negotiable if you intend on creating sustainable growth in your business: the better your information, the better your segmentation, the more effective your offers, the more money you will make. It really works as simply as that.

Relentlessly collecting, organizing, and nurturing the contacts in your database will likely help you reach your sales goals faster than branding or video or almost any other single thing alone.

There are countless ways to use this list of contacts and you will learn all about them shortly but for now having the basics like names, emails, phone numbers, and contact type centralized in one place will cover the 20% of effort that will get you 80% of the results we're looking for.

Done is very much better than perfect in the data arena because we can always circle back to add more information as its discovered. First we just need the ability to communicate.

As one of your most useful tools, getting your list into action is key to accelerating everything else you do, so get going immediately even if you only have 25 people to start.

Frequently Asked List Questions:

"Where's the best place to keep my database?"

The truth is, if you are carrying out the steps you'll be learning soon, you will be collecting leads at a steady pace. In order to put this data to work you will want a tool beyond just a spreadsheet or risk finding yourself struggling to export and import groups of contacts to email servers or physical mailers or other software which can become a nightmare quicker than you think.

Once you have a handle on the information you currently possess, we will want to start looking for a proper C.R.M. or customer relationship management system that fits the way you do business.

FUNNELS 101: Lists, Databases, & Tracking

The obvious options range from Hubspot to Aweber or Keap(formerly Infusionsoft), like I use. But it's important to know that you don't need to spend money to get a healthy database in place and generating money.

"What if I already have a list but it's "bad?"

A list isn't good or bad necessarily, even if you have very low metrics. It's better to think of it more on a scale of healthy or toxic. When something is healthy, you would want to keep doing things to promote it's continued health, right? But when something is toxic or toxified, it's necessary to begin taking steps toward eliminating the toxins and in this case save as many contacts as you can to begin rebuilding a healthy list.

"What about buying a list?"

This is a dangerous space to play in but also potentially very profitable. Like most gray areas, there is a best practices and a "right" way to do it. Overall, an organic list that you build yourself is always preferable to a list that you buy or acquire from someone else. Not to be mistaken with **"affiliate mailing"** *or someone else doing a mailing or broadcast to their list as themselves but on your behalf.*

In the case of buying a list, you'll essentially be taking strangers contact information that you purchase from a 3rd party and contacting them blind. This is risky because getting flagged enough times may get your C.R.M. account disabled, but like most things there are ways to keep this from happening.

"Does everyone I network with belong on my list?"

Not everyone goes on your list and it's so important you don't include everyone you meet. Contacts that don't belong will absolutely skew your metrics and potentially affect your deliverability if you get flagged as junk often enough (although there are ways around this as well).

Insure contacts are either a lead, customer, potential affiliate or partner, before you add them. A bloated list will drag down your numbers and affect your deliverability overall, so be vigilant.

"How are different types of contacts separated?"

*Keep people separate and organized using "**segmentation**."*

*It can be tricky within a spreadsheet sometimes without keeping multiple tabs running with separate lists, but within a proper C.R.M. you'll be able to use "**tags**," lists or a similar mechanic to keep track of who's who and maintain separate conversations or make separate offers.*

You may look at the list of people in your database and think to yourself "well these people aren't going to buy my product or service, so why waste time keeping track of them?"

Keep in mind: Things change. People grow. Circumstances develop. You never know who you've met that may need you months or years later. With a strong, segmented database you can stay T.O.M. (Top of Mind), where someone will see your message at just the right time and take action.

CHAPTER 6

TARGET MARKETING 301:
The Hierarchy of Value

"I'll have what she's having"
(When Harry Met Sally, 1989)

The second step to accurately hitting the right target is identifying your *loyal customers* **"Hierarchy of Value:"** what they find valuable about your business and in what order. We do this by creating a **"value ladder,"** and we'll make our first couple together.

EXAMPLE CASE STUDY:

Customers of a restaurant may value things like food taste, quality, portion size, price, wait time, convenience, atmosphere, presentation, friendliness of staff, alcoholic drink strength, etc. but what are their actual priorities when it comes to their purchasing decisions?

Consider two restaurants:

Restaurant A & Restaurant B...

At **Restaurant A**, many of their *loyals* are willing to drive across town because of how incredible the food is, it's exceptional atmosphere, and strong drinks, even if it's expensive. The portions sizes are small and the waiters tend to be on the snooty side, but who cares? It's trendy!

Restaurant B serves mostly *loyals* who live or work in a two mile radius of their storefront with very fast - affordable options which may not taste as good as fancier places, but you get a whole lot of it and the people working there remember your name.

Both examples can be very successful businesses. Both can make lots of money.

But it's imperative they're crystal clear on who they're best fit to serve and what exactly makes them the best fit for that target. Those are the things that actually drive customers to become loyal to the business. Once you have this information you'll know exactly what buttons to push to bring in more *loyal customers* who will come back and spend more, more often.

Restaurant A may work on getting high reviews from local news stations and papers, they may want to get on their local N.P.R. station or morning blend variant.

Restaurant B may just need to blanket their neighborhood with fliers about a seasonal meal special without ever spending a dime on *major media*.

Both could result in a stack of cash for both business owners.

But if **Restaurant B** had focused on getting time on their local television or radio stations they could have blown their budget by a mile with no returns, because their food just isn't really worth driving across town for.

If **Restaurant A** advertised only in their local area, it's very likely that most of their affluent, trendy, professional audience would have never even known they existed.

Both would be going out of business very soon continuing on that path.

So let's take a look at their different *loyal client's* "**value ladders:**"

RESTAURANT A LOYAL:
Food Quality
Food Taste
Atmosphere
Food Presentation
Alcohol Options
Portion Size
Friendliness of Staff
Price
Convenience

cont.

RESTAURANT B LOYAL:
- Convenience
- Price
- Portion Size
- Food Taste
- Friendliness of Staff
- Food Presentation
- Atmosphere
- Food Quality

But how do you determine what is most valuable to your customer and in what order? Some of these should be obvious, but not necessarily.

Some business owners suffer from a delusion about who they serve. Others are hoping to serve an audience that doesn't reflect their actual loyal base. Both can be catastrophic for your marketing strategy.

There is absolutely no shame in serving someone at a lower price point and not every business needs to be a boutique or charge the highest price in the market. Figure out who you are best fit to serve and serve them with everything you have - it doesn't matter if your business makes custom handmade collectibles or knock off toys for kids whose parents can't afford better. You have to be honest about who you serve and why.

Rank your *loyal customers* value points as accurately as you can. Ask employees or team members to participate and help provide insight in this process. You need as much honesty and experienced input as possible.

TARGET MARKETING 301: The Hierarchy of Value

Study your customers. Who buys from you often? Get to know them. Figure out why they like you best. But try to refrain from asking them directly or giving them something like a questionnaire or survey to fill out - I've seen this tried many times to mixed results.

Some customers tell you what they think you want to hear, others may not know why they do what they do exactly themselves. Either way their direct feedback isn't accurate or useful.

Try to use your collective deductive reasoning to complete this *Value Ladder* for your business. Just know that similar to documentary filmmaking, if a subject is conscious of being studied it will affect the results.

Be aware that audiences change, demographics shift, your business will possibly grow into new targets. There are lots of reasons why, but it's important that you re-evaluate your value ladder at least a couple times a year with fresh eyes. Not doing so can hold you back and force you to miss new opportunities as trends emerge.

CHAPTER 7

SALES 101:
Leads, Whales, and the Simple Sales Formula

"Captain Gardner, I seek the white whale"
(Moby Dick, 1956)

Sales and Marketing are two very different sides of the same coin. Marketing is everything you do to attract and keep a customer, while sales is the interaction where someone actually commits to a purchase or decision to act. Having a marketing system will bring you traffic, but you must be good enough at sales to actually close the deals.

You probably aren't going to become a master salesperson over night but thankfully when you have the **simple sales formula,** it's actually simple:

Offer + Lead + Sales Process = Revenue

Put the right offer in front of the right qualified lead with the right message and they will allow you to solve their problem. When you skillfully combine these three sales chemicals together in the right concentrations, the yield is a purchase. That doesn't necessarily insure long term success, but it's a great start.

Offer: Beyond just "what you sell," is "what EXACTLY are you selling?" Pick something that you're poised to move immediately and set an enticing price. Yes, if during the sales process the lead decides to buy something other than what you went into the conversation expecting, that's outstanding too, but for the process of directed sales efforts it's best to begin with a particular offer or product in mind.

- You aren't just selling business coaching, you are offering your $2997 3-month business building course.

- You aren't just selling your HVAC services, you're offering a new hypoallergenic home air filter package for $475.

- You aren't just selling maid services, you're letting them know you have a spring deep-clean promotion for $399.

Step one is deciding exactly what you should offer your contacts right now to get your new sales efforts rolling.

LEAD: Not who you want to sell to in the future, but who can you sell to right now? It's a good time to review your contact database for anyone who may value this deal. If you've completed step one and you have an offer in hand, ask yourself who you have access to that's the right fit.

Do you have 50 customers you've helped in the past who are qualified to buy this new offer? Create a sales process for them, they are now leads.

Used the *target map* and *value ladder* to identify where new potential *loyal customers* are hanging out? Figure out how to best earn their eyeballs and get out there.

Met 50 qualified people in the last 3 months at networking events who can buy this product? They are leads for this offer now too.

Pull these viable contacts into their own list or tag them in your *C.R.M.* or add them to the first step of your **"sales pipeline"** so that you can begin reaching out to them about your offer.

SALES PROCESS:

> FACT: All Successful Sales Conversations are Grounded in Solving Your Customers Pain Better Than Anyone Or Anything Else.

Armed with an offer and a list of leads for said offer, let's start selling!

The **"sales process"** is literally any process in which you persuade someone to take action. Yours doesn't have to be a complicated one, nor does it have to be perfect but it does have to be well planned. Like everything you are going to be mapping and constructing as you grow, it will get better over time.

There are advanced sales processes and simple ones.

Some include emails and texts and campaigns and content, but depending on your business you may not need to rely solely on those more advanced tools. Often simpler is better, especially if your sales department needs to generate cash flow quickly.

There is nothing wrong with a 1-step sales process if it works and you see them all the time for a reason: the contractors at Costco offer you a sample, delivers a **"quick-pitch"** and asks you to buy, simple as that. Some people do, others might later, most won't. That's a sales process. Not a graceful one, but obviously it works for their particular volume model and that's something you should never forget: you need to have a sales process that is tailored for your audience, your overall marketing model and the type of traffic you are approaching.

What actual **"engagements"** does it take for someone to make a decision to purchase your product? Once you have established that, it's time to get to work becoming visible.

I'm not above asking a stranger at the mall to buy fashion coaching services from my client, I'm not afraid to pick up the phone and call old contacts to sell them my new product. You can't be either. This is where you get in front of your target no matter what it takes.

So does it take a phone call? Does it take an in person discussion? *A quick-pitch*? Will they buy from an online store? Where exactly do these people say "yes" or "no?" This is your **"sales choke,:"** or (**"choke point"**) the point of contact in which your average lead will decide to purchase the product being offered or not; it's where the rubber meets the sales road. Once you have it identified, focus on driving as many leads to this *choke point* as efficiently as possible while minimizing distractions along the way.

If it's a physical location that your leads are congregating in then figure out how to become more visible there as soon as possible. If they are professional contacts you may need to find them on LinkedIn or jump on the phone and start reaching out one by one.

> *Your "**conversion rate**" is the ratio of contacts that go from one step to the next in any particular part of the sales process, measured in percent. If you send a sales email and 100 people open it but 10 purchase, you converted at 10%. If you asked 50 leads to come to a workshop and 12 show up, that's a 24% conversion. Pretty simple, right?*
>
> *You will want to be keeping track of these numbers more and more as you grow if you aren't already.*

With these three steps in motion you will need to begin generating new leads to get to more "yes's."

Leads are the one consistent element of all businesses in all industries. But not all leads are equal… they come in three primary flavors:

"**Cold Leads**" are prospects who usually don't know you from a stranger off the street or have only had a brief interaction with your business. You'll usually need to "**educate**" and *initiate* these people before they are ready to spend any serious money with you. Start with an offer they can't refuse to begin building your relationship. Lead with value. Expect an extended sales cycle.

"**Warm Leads**" know who you are and what you do, but either haven't purchased anything from you, spent only a small amount, or haven't purchased in longer than

9-months (can also include referral contacts who trust someone that's recommended you). These people may be ready to buy with the right offer much more often than a cold lead but you may need to gently remind them about the value you provide before they're ready for action.

Hot Leads" are people already know, love, and trust you. These are your customers, *loyals*, and anyone who has made significant purchases with you in the last 180 days. The Hot Leads sales cycle should be the quickest. Pick up the phone or send an email with a new offer that's right for them and expect a positive response. Your hot leads are the most likely to buy without objections.

In my databases I always choose to distinguish between Hot, Warm, and Cold leads clearly with a tag or segmentation because of just how different the *conversion* rates are for each of the groups.

But beyond just Hot, Warm, and Cold traffic, there is one more type of lead that you need to be prepared for:

"WHALES:"

Although I'm not the hunting type and would certainly never hunt an actual whale, the truth is it's the best term for the job, so here we go.

The top 20% of the top 20%, *whales* are big spenders who are exactly the right fit for what you do. A business may sell coaching courses as their main product but a whale wants to spend big money to have you solve the whole problem for them top to bottom. They might want to fly you out to work with them one on one. You should

SALES 101: Leads, Whales, and the Simple Sales Formula

never stop hunting whales in your business.

Whales don't care about cost, they care about results. If a whale is saying your offer is too expensive, they either aren't a whale or they aren't convinced of the results.

Every industry has its whales: A landscaping business can land an H.O.A. contract for dozens of properties. A clothing company can secure influential market leaders or wholesalers instead of just their online or retail traffic. A nail salon can land the business of a retirement community and end up doing the nails of hundreds of seniors every month on top of the people who already come to them. These prospects are worth hundreds or thousands or hundreds of thousands of dollars a year or more.

Whales can shift the momentum of your business in a moment so keep a sea-eye open and a harpoon ready, but I'm not promising I won't call you Ishmael.

As you continue to grow and segment your database with special offers for all of your new and future customers, remember to have an established path for each of these types of leads so that none of them catch you off guard when they emerge.

But now that your familiar with the waters around leads, you'll need to tackle another current where your traffic is going to be...

CHAPTER 8

SOCIAL MEDIA 101:
The "YOU" Show

"Frankly, my dear, I don't give a damn"
(Gone With the Wind, 1939)

People absorb you not just through the language you use on your website, but also your video, your emails, your promotional materials, and everything else you're using to communicate. First of all, it's important to re-emphasize just how much words matter. Story matters. Your journey matters - and it all shines brightest on social media.

Everyone knows everyone again: The world is different than it was just a generation ago and has become much more like that of our grandparents and great-grandparents with a small-town mentality firmly at play. The advent and rise of social media has made our professional reputations very public, allowing anyone to find you in a moments notice with no effort at all. It's so important you're represented properly and that only takes a couple of hours each week if you are committed to the right game plan... *That's only minutes a day.*

It obviously wasn't always this way, but if you're marketing a successful operation going forward without an active social media persona on at least one platform, you're in for an uphill battle the whole way.

Almost certainly, your competition is actively investing time and resources into their social media presence and you can be assured that it'll absolutely be a determining factor for at least some of your potential customers, so let's attack your competition directly out of the gate with some ground work.

The good news is this: you don't have to be better or flashier than your competition to win the sale in social media, you just can't not be there when someone looks you up. With me?

For many people, the term *"social media marketing"* is a shorthand way to describe any activity in places like Facebook or Twitter for their business. And sure, they can be great for showing up where your targets are hanging out in theory, but there's more to it than that. On a deeper level, **<u>social media marketing</u>**" should be anchored around documenting you solving the problem you solve. This is how you influence people's perception of your overall value and grow authority over time. It's not really about how many likes you are getting necessarily, it's about how many sales you are driving and that is directly tied to the authority you've built through consistent activity.

Success hangs largely on one very important question from now on: *Did you do your social media homework?*

Your business' Facebook page is the very next thing you need to develop after a functional list.

In reality, most new potential customers who encounter your business will only spend about 30-45 seconds initially **<u>scrolling</u>**," or looking through your online presence, before making a gut decision on whether they will take the next step. This is the **<u>digital legitimacy test</u>**," and passing it can be as easy as keeping even basic, regular, relevant activity on your profiles over time. Doing so allows you to retain around 80% of these "*second-look skeptics*" and that will keep you competing with the big guys as you grow into a more robust social media presence. This is a powerful tactic for **<u>intro-preneurs</u>**" or anyone new to marketing their business online.

For most small businesses, the majority of those people visiting your social media profile will be those you have met or connected with in another capacity who are only looking you over to see if you are who you say you are. Yes, there are many people driving tons of fresh traffic from their social media accounts but if you are new to this arena, focus on getting enough content to pass this *digital legitimacy test* first - it'll make a world of difference in your conversion rate faster than you think.

It's important to understand that not every business needs to be on every social media platform. Not everybody needs an Instagram, and a Twitter, and a Reddit, and a Snapchat, and a Pinterest, but you should aspire to be present on at least two or three (one being Facebook) to pass the Digital Legitimacy Test; but don't worry, it's not anywhere as difficult as it seems.

SOCIAL MEDIA SURVIVAL TACTIC: documentation vs. content creation

Social media is a beast that must be fed content in order to stay relevant and keep your audience engaged.

This is often a place where entrepreneurs, business owners, and marketers get stuck. How and where do you come up with all this content, especially when you're new to the whole process?

We'll be learning later in the book how to create high quality **"content marketing,"** but for this introduction the important thing for you to remember is this: documenting your journey is infinitely cheaper and more effective than going out to create a professional video or a great graphic with a clever *copy* laid over it just right.

*But **how** exactly do you create captivating content without hiring staff?*

Every day in your business, you should be working with the people you serve to solve the problem you solve, right? You are simply going to start flipping on your camera and documenting yourself in the midst of doing so. The best solutions are often the simplest and I assure you, this is the content that your future customers want to see more than anything. You in action. Welcome to **"docu-content:"**

A glass company can share videos of technicians on location fixing a piece of glass along with a minute or two about something like why it's so important not to let your cracks go because they can randomly shatter without warning.

A restaurant or food truck should be posting video of

their chef preparing the meal of the day along with talking about things like how their food is so fresh.

A coach could set up a tripod to record a couple minutes of leading a workshop, or even a snippet of working with someone one on one along with a small message to show the impact of what they are doing.

A specialty-pharmacy can shoot a video of someone working with supplements and discussing the best ways to get more absorption of nutrients.

An e-commerce store can post a video of a new limited shipment they have along with some details about what makes it so special.

...The list is endless within your typical work week.

Next, post this content to your Facebook Business page and then share it on your personal page. Now you are earning eyeballs. Rinse and repeat.

There are almost no industries where this strategy can't be implemented and I assure you that it's the most affordable way to get your businesses social media up to speed while replacing thousands and thousands of dollars in content creation.

The easiest content you can create comes from the value you provide to your customers. Take photos of products, of meetings with clients, of the production process, befores and afters, of new openings, handshakes, happy customers and yourself in the mix every day. This goes back to the power of your journey in the marketing process.

It's way better to have ten times more media of your journey than you need. Taking digital photos and videos costs you nothing but can be invaluable later when it comes to your business's content strategy and in the hands of the right professional, those pieces can become captivating videos very affordably - so again, more is better when it comes to content.

In today's social media market, people want to know who they are working with and the easiest way to do that is to be real. Yes, polished graphics and great design will do wonders but don't forget to include the human element of your business, especially here in your social media.

There are many companies and businesses that command their followers through the photos and videos they take of their journey every day without ever stepping into a studio and you can too.

One of my favorite Facebook business personalities actually sells insurance policies, arguably one of the most boring products to many people. He documents his daily journey and it becomes easy to see how much he cares and does for the people that depend on him. He does **"Facebook LIVE"** videos regularly, chats with team members, raps in the car on the drive home from helping customers, on his lunch break, motivating while filling out papers late in the office, at the gym, etc. Whether good or bad, his successes and failures are always an inspiration to me as a business owner because he's an expert, he's real but more importantly for him, he's **"indoctrinated"** me to his brand by posting this *docu-content* consistently over time. If he offered coverage in California where I live, I would be a proud customer of his without a doubt. That's the power of sharing a strong journey: you become more than just the thing that you do.

There's a version of this that is right for your business and best of all, when you are doing it right, it feels effortless.

Here's the winning recipe for compelling social media *docu-content* posts:

1. **Establish a problem your audience has**
2. **Show your business fixing it**
3. **Include a useful or interesting piece of info**
4. **Provide at least one way that your business does this better than anyone else**
5. **Give them the opportunity to engage**

Obviously there are ways to improve on this formula once you have mastered these five basic pieces, but for now - if you can manage to hit these marks in 2-5 minutes just a few times weekly, I bet you won't recognize the influence and **"authority"** your page will be commanding in just a couple months.

Introduction to Facebook Marketing:

First, it's important to be clear on one fact: a Facebook Business page is not a personal Facebook page.

One more time for everyone in the back: a business page is not the same thing as having a personal Facebook page.

What's the difference? A regular, or standard personal Facebook page, is used for sharing your information online and a Facebook Business page is a page used for marketing to people using their personal Facebook pages. One is an information target, and the other is a tool used for catching people sharing that information. One is a fish and the other is a fishing pole.

They are different for very many reasons but let's focus on the big ones: A Personal Facebook Page gets "friends." A Business page gets "likes." One gets *"views"* the other gets *"reach."* A personal page gets access to their friends feeds automatically, where your business page has to earn exposure in one of two ways, purchasing advertising space or through activity generated on your posts. This should be incredibly clear at the beginning for a couple reasons, mainly because it's easy for the uninitiated to misunderstand the Facebook business page rules, but also because if Facebook catches you running a business through a personal page they will lock your account and you will lose everything you've built - unfortunately I've seen it happen first hand.

While it's true that Facebook's influence is in flux due to many factors, Facebook is poised to be the standard for social media presence into the foreseeable future and that means you need to be there regardless of what happens in the news. Mature demographics and others are on Facebook religiously and are very susceptible to influence, so don't skip it.

But what other social media platforms are right for your audience? There is no right answer for every business so you will need to make that judgment yourself as the *Chief Marketer*.

Firstly, ask yourself whether or not your audience engages with your brand visually.

Do you deal in visually engaging things like clothing, photography, or other things that have elements of design?

If so, *Instagram* and *Snapchat* are likely great bets. Do your clients commonly have frequently asked questions? Twitter is a great way to jump in and keep conversations going without relying on too many visuals.

Businesses in some industries may find it difficult to come up with engaging candid photographs on a regular basis so they may want to stick to more text or video based social media sites unless they are prepared to create original *content*, which can potentially be expensive.

Although more activity is certainly better than less, investing in the wrong social media platforms can lead to wasted resources managing a bunch of *content* that may just fall flat.

If the thought of keeping up all the different social media platforms you need scares you, you're not alone. Social media can be time consuming and for that reason, expensive. The tactic many people turn to for keeping their platforms current is **"social media integration."**

Social media integration is the process of sharing one piece of *content* on several different platforms. This alleviates much of the burden of creating tons of *content* but be careful with this strategy: it only works if you understand and exploit the differences between the platforms and the audiences who are hanging out there.

You wouldn't want to just go sending your Facebook posts automatically to *Twitter*, *Instagram*, *LinkedIn*, *Reddit*, etc, without double checking the content and making appropriate adjustments to fit the platform you are sharing on - you've been warned.

Fight the urge to become overwhelmed by focusing

on just your next pieces of content. Success with your social media is possible no matter the industry you are in, how comfortable you are with technology, or your budget as long as you are willing to commit to baby steps on a regular basis. One post at a time.

Challenge yourself to start recording and sharing the work you do today!

Social Media FAQs:

"How long should a Facebook post be?"

If it's pure text, try not to go past 300 words. If you find yourself getting to that length, you may want to consider writing a blog post on your website instead, then share it to Facebook along with a preview to get people engaged.

"How often should I post?"

The obvious answer is - as often as possible. But by posting or specifically docu-posting twice to three times a week, you will have an impressive account with plenty of great content to pass a digital legitimacy test before you know it. If you don't have a social media presence on Facebook yet, challenge yourself to put up at least one new thing every day for 30 days - even if it is just a photo or a curated share. Remember that social media is a marathon, not a sprint. Your posts will become cumulatively more valuable over time.

"

SOCIAL MEDIA 101: The "YOU" Show

What is "Social Reputation Management?'"

Social media is one of, if not the first thing potential customers will look at after meeting you and so your online reputation is important. This term is thrown around a lot by people who are trying to sell a service, so be careful how you approach the subject of Social Reputation Management.

Google yourself and see if you find anything you wouldn't want a client to see and address it directly. For most businesses, this should be enough to keep you in the clear but that's not to say your social reputation shouldn't be checked regularly for negative activity.

"Is LinkedIn a waste of time?"

Possibly, although probably not. Not every social media platform is the right fit for every business but chances are you should be showing up on LinkedIn as it's the social media network for professionals. Even if you don't specifically serve the business community it will be good for your networking and collaboration efforts as you grow. Develop a LinkedIn account if only for the purpose of networking with peers who may have access to resources or audiences you need, and check in every week or two at the very least.

"Bonus Tactic"

PARETO'S PRODUCTIVITY (THE POWER HOUR):

Life in business is reliably hectic at times and often that's the only thing you can count on. You will have to schedule times for laser focus and productive Zen if you're going to fight through those daily distractions and keep moving forward toward your more important goals; otherwise they will beat you.

During a *power hour* you're investing 60-minutes of time toward a singular focus and refusing to allow interruptions.

A **"power hour"** is a full hour dedicated to solving one problem, attacking one issue, completing one task, or finishing one project.

Power hours can be the most useful productivity tool you have if you can just follow the rules:

1. Remove noise: Turn off your phone, close all non-related browser windows, have all calls and messages held, do your best to make sure your space is quiet.

2. Prepare: Have everything you need to survive taken care of for the next 60-minutes. Bathroom, water, coffee, snacks, pen, computer, and phone charger, have no reason to leave the room

3. Set a timer: The counting down clock in eyesight can keep you focused when the mind wants to wander.

4. Stay in the room: Entering or exiting a door frame will break the power and it's always difficult to find the same rhythm again.

5. EXECUTE: Until the timer ends, even if the building burns around you, finish.

60-minutes is the perfect window for accomplishing that thing of consequence without allowing you space to get bored, but you have to manage each minute.

Finish the major task of the day without circumstances pulling you away. Single big steps, one hour at a time with a power hour.

CHAPTER 9

NETWORKING 101:
Leads, Leaders, & Buried Treasure

"This is the beginning of a beautiful friendship"
(Casablanca, 1942)

Social Media activity isn't a substitute for actual networking. That fact is worthy of its own chapter.

With rare exception, the *Chief Marketer* of your business should be networking in person around your local community at least two or three times a month, and that's at the very least.

Every single week there are clubs, organizations, groups, and others meeting and connecting. All full of future customers, partners and more that are within driving distance.

Face to face networking is still the most reliable way to expand your local visibility, meet new potential partners, and genuinely connect with the community influencers and leaders in your own backyard. Come prepared and you might even pick up some great new business.

These people often have access to networks of their own and can help you get in front of eyeballs you otherwise wouldn't have access to, so play your cards right with everyone you meet. But it all starts with your commitment to go out and hunt for them.

Know more people, do more business. Not exactly revolutionary, but a fact nonetheless.

Obviously there's more at play, but if you let this general principle guide you, you'll always have strong local resources and support at your fingertips; whether that means partners, *affiliates,* or group organizers that can get you far more exposure than you'd manage alone.

Treasure Hunt: You never know who's in the room with you when you go to a new networking group.

If your target is business to business, don't underestimate the power of memberships in professional groups, clubs, associations and organizations like local business breakfasts, user groups, golf clubs, toastmasters, etc. The "good ol' boys" club is a factor and you can be a member whether a man or a woman. You only have to be willing to show up, get close and play the game,

More recently, the website Meetup.com has gotten into the networking mix with Eventbrite and Facebook and is a great place to find audiences of a wide range of interests. If you haven't visited the site yet, take a few minutes out of your day and look it over. Find groups that center around things that your target client would be interested in attending and join them.

You can fill your professional social calendar with great opportunities to network in almost no time. All you need is a rinse and repeat plan.

If you are new to an area, either because you've moved or found yourself in a new endeavor, the best thing to do is begin getting properly connected. Even if you've only attended a few meetings you will have quite a few local, qualified contacts for your database - there's no excuse for not knowing the right people in your city anymore.

Every month, community organizations like social mixers, sports groups, PTAs, groups for working mothers, professionals of every trade or interest and so many more are full of your potential customers and they're meeting all around you, all the time. So use this knowledge to your advantage while plugging into the community at the same time.

You likely didn't get to where you are without learning how to network at least semi-effectively, but everyone can always be better so here's a lay of the land:

"The 10 Commandments of Networking Events:"

1. **Be on time** - If being on time is a challenge for you, plan to arrive to networking events early. Being late is a real deal breaker for some sticklers, whereas showing up early means possibly getting face time with the organizer if you offer to help set up, which is always a power move.

2. **Fit in** - Don't be the only person somewhere in jeans,

the same goes for a polo shirt or blouse equivalent. But you also don't want to be overdressed for a gathering. If in doubt, check their social media or group page and see what others wore to past events.

3. **Stand out** - For the right reasons of course. Be enthusiastic. Be funny. Be knowledgeable. Be sharp.

4. **Nail Your introduction** - Having a confident introduction is the difference between instant authority or quick confusion. A little practice goes a long way. If in doubt, begin with "*My name is ABC and people hire me to help them XYZ.*" It's a great formula to get the conversation started right. This isn't a magic power that some have and others don't, you have to work at it to get good. Practice as often as possible until you are comfortable and getting results.

5. **Be prepared** - Business cards are a must. Self designed mini fliers are acceptable in a pinch, but never be the person who has to write their number down for a qualified lead on a napkin.

6. **Be enthusiastic** - Have something to be excited about. What's the biggest win your business has had recently? What are you looking forward to? Enthusasm is contagious and having something to share with others will give you a boosted magnetism while encouraging them to reciprocate.

7. **Be present** - Don't be on your phone. Don't be distracted. Participate full out. Make eye contact. Keep your head up. Challenge yourself to have a conversation with everyone in the room. Be helpful. All of these things lead to a powerful and attractive

presence at any event.

8. **Have a "biggest need"** - You never know when you are going to get the opportunity to talk to someone who can give you exactly what you need. If you always show up with something in your mind ready to share, you are much more likely to articulate it to others and way more likely to find a solution. You can't be afraid to put it out there. Obviously you won't want to share your need with everyone you meet but when appropriate tell someone you're connecting with what you are looking for or working on in your business; they will often try to find ways to help, it's human nature.

9. **Have your calendar open** - When you meet someone that is the right fit, don't wait around. Ask them if they have their phone on them (they do). Open your calendar, and schedule your next conversation or step with them right then and there. This is the cleanest way to take advantage of a good connection on the spot.

10. **Be persistent** - Everyone you meet should get an email, note, or follow up from you in some way so you can add them to your database and begin the appropriate sales cycle. This will make you very likable and will further insure that any potential deals don't fall through the cracks.

"The Three Strike Networking Rule:"

The 10 Commandments of Networking are important to remember for anyone new to the world of networking functions. Be mindful, these rules aren't arbitrary. The group mentality is real. If a new attendee of an event breaks three or more of any of these rules the group will notice and that person will garner a collective negative response, so break them at your own peril.

Networking FAQ: Should I join a networking group?

Maybe. But though attending groups and meetings as a guest can be great for quickly expanding local reach, joining a certain group as a member will have its own benefits, resources, and obligations. Don't rush into something just because they put pressure on you to join, because they often will.

Think of it like dating: see what's out there before picking the right one. It's OK to say no to someone who's not the right fit. There are plenty of opportunities out there and depending on the area you live in, potentially hundreds of rooms filled with people who are perfect for you. So ask, is worth it to invest in seeing these same people on a regular basis? It might be. Are the fees and dues worth the return on investment? Possibly. How much time are you spending at functions? Will that investment generate real money in your business? Answer these questions before choosing.

If you do decide to join a networking group: participate in their volunteer efforts in a big way. If they don't have one, spearhead it. Not only is this our businesses obligation to the community but it's one of the best things you can do as a market leader. Leaders give, so give and become a leader - it's all relative.

People who see you more often and have a regular positive experience will tend to want to work with you.

"Dodge the Dodge:"

It's happened to the best of us... We're having a conversation with someone we're sure we'll do business with and get their card with the old "Great, I'm so glad we met. I'm going to call you first thing tomorrow." But tomorrow comes and no matter what you do or how many times you do it all you get is dead air. You've been *dodged*.

Even if your lead really connected with you as a person the truth is they saw a sales pitch coming and even though they may completely need what you do, they didn't have the capacity for it right then - despite being exactly the right fit to solve their pain.

But how do you make sure the next stage actually happens?

Most people will keep their social obligations, so let's tie our sales process into their integrity. Make an appointment when someone is right in front of you because it makes it awkward for them to say no. So if you're sure this is someone you want that next conversation with, *dodge the dodge* with an appointment. Look them right in the eye and ask for permission to follow up - that way you are never imposing when you do. As you're wrapping up a conversation, ask something like "Hey, so it's cool if we talk on Monday, right? Great, what time is good? Is this your best email?"

Then enter it into your calendar and send them a digital invitation right then and there - this way you aren't putting yourself in a position of tracking people down and hoping for the best, you're showing up for your appointment. People dodge sales calls, they rarely dodge confirmed appointments, especially with peers and professionals.

Always give yourself a next step appointment when confronted with opportunity for a profitable conversation.

The "**Lean In:**" this tactic gets people to genuinely inquire about your business instead of just waiting to talk.

Networking events are notorious for activities that pair you up with other attendees to discuss topical subjects and it's almost always a total waste of time. Let's use these exercises to learn as much about our partners as possible and find out how they can fit into our business without being "**salesy**" like everyone else.

Most people just use these opportunities to talk at whoever is across from them and rarely are they there to listen, so instead consider using the whole time you're given to talk about the other person and what they are doing. Then, if it feels right, begin softly leading them toward the topic of the problem you solve. They won't see it coming. If you are given three minutes each, let them go first and then just keep asking relevant questions through your time. People will usually overshare if you let them and then feel the need to compensate after they catch themselves.

I learned this effect by accident. I genuinely enjoy hearing about people's businesses and their plans and goals, so sometimes I would get caught up talking all about them and before I knew it, the organizer would call time and I'd get a familiar look... a little embarrassment. My partner realized she'd spent the whole time talking about herself and wanted to give me the opportunity to share too, so I suggested we have a call or meet for coffee later and she really couldn't say no, nor did she want to. Boom, lead converted, and later sale made.

Spend your allotted time laser focused on the other person. If they aren't a sociopath, soon they'll naturally want to reciprocate and want to know everything about what you do too. But because you've been such a good listener, they will naturally like you and want to find ways to help you grow your business beyond being a customer. When you're targeting properly these people become *loyal customers* very easily if they are qualified in the first place. This is a great way to use the social contract effectively while being a conscious marketer and a good friend, but you can't fake it. You'll actually have to connect if you're going to collect the treasure that's right in front of you.

CHAPTER 10

FUNNELS 201:
Blueprints, High-Touch, & Commitment

"Mrs. Robinson, you're trying to seduce me, aren't you?" (The Graduate, 1967)

Funnels 201 has less to do with bots, software or technology and everything to do with creating the blueprints your company will follow to consistently make specific sales over and over. Mapping the distinct instructions for reliably taking new qualified leads through a successful *sales journey* from beginning to end with zero guesswork - that's the DNA of functional **"marketing automation."**

If you're thinking of automation as an invasive technical process your business has to undergo similar to surgery, you will be overwhelmed in no time and likely have a tough experience overall. Especially if you are planning on building the system yourself, focus on each piece and how it alleviates a particular challenge until you have a solid foundation in place beneath you. One step at a time.

"Systems reduce cost and labor."

But they're also the most effective way to make sure everyone's getting the same outstanding experience every time while also being certain you're providing each opportunity the highest likelihood of becoming a sale.

Example Case Study: I am going to a networking event and want to sell my flagship $6997 Small-Business Accelerator where we build clients a sexy new WordPress website and a custom sales system to handle their new traffic.

I know that I may meet 5, 10, 20 or more qualified cold leads who are a great fit for the package and I need to make the most of each one.

I also know that my *sales choke point* for the product isn't a *quick-pitch* at this networking event at all, it's a longer face to face conversation either in person or over web-conference where I can learn more about them and we can focus on their business without distraction.

So rather than hitting the qualified leads in the room with a sales offer or playing phone tag forever, I'm going to strategically engineer the sales steps beforehand to make sure that everyone receives great *education* and *initiation* while gently but steadily pushing all of them to the conversation where they're presented with the purchase –

but that begins with collecting their contact information so it can be added to the database appropriately and begin the sales cycle. That's the conversion I'm really counting on.

"**Education**" is the process of showing someone how your specific product is going to make their life better. Your lead must be crystal clear on why they need what you are offering.

"**Initiation**" is establishing to a lead who you are and what gives your business the authority to solve their problem. Your lead must believe that you are the best person *AND* company to serve them.

Ideally the educating and initiating happens through follow-up immediately after meeting your lead, preferably through a series of thoughtfully constructed emails and outreach, possibly with a blend of *content* and social media *engagement* mixed in.

Although it's completely possible that someone at the event needs a marketing rebuild bad enough to buy it right there and then, knowing the sales cycle as I do, it's more likely the majority will need at least one more conversation before they know me and my company well enough for them to make a purchasing decision and that means some *nurture* or follow up is in order.

"**Nurture**" is the act of educating, initiating and providing value to someone over time until they are ready to act, whether that be later today or a year from now.

So again, even though it is totally possible that someone says "yes" in the room, and it does happen, it's way more likely that I'll need to add them to a *sales pipeline* within my list for more follow up to get to that next conversation efficiently - so that's where I'm going to focus.

Having a sales system actually takes the pressure off of me as the *Chief Marketer* to close deals at that exact moment, allowing me to focus on connecting, qualifying and collecting more valuable leads in the room.

But what would the nurture process look like for the upcoming event from this example?

Since I'm meeting all of these leads at the same location and qualifying them for the same product, it's only logical to map a singular journey for everyone to travel upfront that draws them toward the choke point over multiple emails, texts and calls in case they don't respond right away.

The benefit being that with the right prework and mapping you can anticipate your incoming leads and be ready with great follow up so that you won't have to create it on the fly where you risk valuable opportunities falling through the cracks. Remember: Systems reduce cost and labor.

What do you do if they don't respond to the first follow up? Or the second? Or the third? People's lives are busy and there are thousands of reasons someone might not respond right away; it certainly doesn't mean that they aren't interested, or that they aren't the right fi\ - they wouldn't have given you their contact info otherwise. You just need to keep the conversation active until they engage. This series of communications to get someone to take action is a Sales Journey or **"campaign"** and it happens over time to keep reminding a prospective customer that you are the right person at the right company with the right product to solve their pain.

By creating this blueprint of the sales journey beforehand with multiple touch-points I'll know that every single person will have a great experience with a warm welcome and relevant content without me worrying about who is where; freeing me up to focus on closing deals and doing what I do best.

(Process) A new lead met at Networking Event may experience a *campaign* like this:

1. Send email 1 (Greeting) → *Wait 24 hours* →
2. Send email 2 (w/value content) → *Wait 15 min* →
3. Send text to look for email 2 → *Wait 48 hours* →
4. Send email 3 (Reminder) → *Wait 24 hours* →
5. Phone call to confirm their email address. → *etc.*

These are just the few first steps but this will continue until they book a conversation with me and at that point this process ends and another begins; more about that soon.

If a good number of leads I put into my system will take me up on my first offer to have a discovery/sales call, what happens to the ones who don't? Depending on the industry, on average it can take as many as 8 to 14 touches or more before a new qualified lead makes a decision to give you a chance, so it's incredibly important you don't stop after the first try.

(A "**touch**" is an interaction and can include anything from an in-person encounter, a conversation, an email, ad, content a phone call, a text, a testimonial, or any other direct exposure to your business.)

This is more important than what *C.R.M.* you choose - it's the actual foundation of automation. Yes, it takes software and integration and technology to make all these processes happen automatically and that stuff can be cumbersome and confusing if you aren't software savvy, but you'll be able to make it all work if you just understand these basic fundamentals first.

The next chapter introduces you to content and copywriting but here is an example of a welcome email that works incredibly well in my typical event automation:

Subject: *Follow up from* **NAME OF THE EVENT**

Body: *Hey,* **NAME OF CONTACT***! It's Ashley from the* **NAME OF THE EVENT***. How are you???*
It was really great meeting you and I think It's important we connect sooner rather than later.
I know you mentioned you're in the process of doing some big things with **NAME OF BUSINESS** *and I want to hear more about it.*
C.T.A.: *Call or text me when you have some time, OR*
You can get to my calendar right here:
LINK TO CALENDAR

Salutation*: Keep it up!*

*Ashley Wilkes Webber (***PHONE NUMBER***)*

P.S.*: I'd love to stay connected on Facebook. This is my page: CLICK HERE*

Notice how even though the email is automated, it's designed to sound like it was written just to one person and it works for almost everybody I'm going to meet, but best of all, my new map works for every networking event I go to from now on. All I need to do is swap the names. That makes it very powerful for getting batches of new leads to respond with minimal effort. You can learn how to write these for your sales system too with the *H.T.C.M. (High Touch Conversational Marketing)* philosophy," but before you go writing the follow up emails and text, you need to map the journey you want prospects to experience and be clear on how they get to the *choke point* from beginning to end. Don't forget this mapping step.

The "High Touch Conversational Marketing Method (H.T.C.M.):"

The process of keeping in touch very regularly with valuable *content* in a casual, conversational tone until the prospect is ready to act. Developed over years of working with hundreds and hundreds of businesses across many industries, *H.T.C.M.* is the best groundwork I've found for building funnels and writing sales campaigns every single day.

This is in direct contrast to *broadcast marketing* or other types of traditional long-form sales formats that can turn off many audiences by being too "salesy."

"**Broadcast marketing:**" The practice of blanketing

an audience with a general message regardless of who they are, hoping to hit qualified customers; the epitome of speaking to everyone versus one particular target. Broadcast marketing is highly competitive and therefore both notoriously expensive and often relatively ineffective when you look at the metrics. But that doesn't mean it isn't the right fit for certain businesses depending on their market and where they are in their growth plan.

Instead of speaking to your leads like every other business, talk to them like a really good friend would. That's very much how your sales follow up should be - A good friend casually reaching out to someone they like, about something they both find valuable. It's difference of talking *with* someone instead of talking *at* them...

H.T.C.M. Examples:

"Hey, **Darin**! How are you?? I don't know if you've been on my Facebook page today but I got these new sunglasses in stock and they are definitely your style. Take a look and tell me if I'm crazy - click here."

"Hi there, **Janel**! I know it's been a couple weeks since we were in touch but I'm doing a webinar on 7-figure funnels Thursday and I totally think you should be there if you are still working hard on **NAME OF BUSINESS.** Let me know you can make it

-Register here."

"Oh wow, **Usvaldo**... Did you know that every year thousands of kids like ours are getting sick because of dirty air filters left in the house?? Check out this research attached. I don't know what you have going on this week but I'd love to send someone over to inspect your place? I'll have them throw some fresh filters in the truck just in case you are ready for a *switch (with a special deal of course). Just call Becky at the office or reply here."*

With *H.T.C.M.*, you're going to reach out and touch your target often with simple, non-threatening info, offers, updates and invitations until they find themselves at the *choke point*. Your objective is to encourage the target to feel like you aren't driving a sale at all. You are passionate, enthusiastic and excited to be connected with them. As their trusted expert in your field, it's your job to ensure they are informed and have everything they need. That's the "conversational" element of this equation.

If you have done a good job making sure that you've cultivated the right type of leads in the first place and you are *speaking your customers language*, you'll eventually get a steady percentage of your audience to take you up on your offers. It's simply a matter of staying *top of mind* in their *inbox*, on their phones, or in front of their eyeballs however you can until they say "yes." That is the "high-touch" element.

FACT: When you look into an established company's sales numbers you'll find that there's an average number of touches or exposures a lead usually needs from their business before they make a purchasing decision for any particular offer; this is known as your *offer frequency*.

"**Offer frequency**" is the average number of touches or exposures that a lead has to have over time before they're ready to take action.

Yes, some will buy sooner and others may take a little longer; but if you determine that the average number of times a qualified lead needs to encounter your offer is 7.4 touches before they decide to buy or act, then it simply becomes a question of how we best get in front of them that many times before expecting a certain number of those to take you up on your offer.

Using your data to project how many sales or actions you will receive from a particular campaign or effort is known as **"forecasting"** and is an important part of using automated systems in your businesses growth plan.

If you know your numbers, stay focused on generating qualified leads that fit your *target map,* and make sure that your high-touch sales process is being adhered to, you can absolutely expect to increase revenues.

> **5 Simple tips for effectively using *H.T.C.M.*:**
> 1. Communicate in 1st person: "I" & "Me" when possible as opposed to "Us" & "We."
>
> 2. Be Frequent: Stay Top of Mind.
>
> 3. Be Conversational: Don't sound like their English professor or a corporate suit.
>
> 4. Be concise: Don't use ten words when five will do.
>
> 5. Don't be "salesy:" Stay away from jargon and anything you'd hear in a car commercial.

Escalation of Commitment:

When you meet someone new you might be interested in dating, hopefully you ask them out on a first date before trying to get them to go home with you straight from Barnes & Noble. You could and it might work...

but chances are it's going to come off as way too strong.

Your sales relationships work very much the same way. When we meet the perfect prospect whether they are online or in person, we want to gather information and explore the relationship before jumping to any conclusions about where this whole thing is going. You don't want to waste valuable time on somebody who's not on the market or you just plain aren't compatible with. That's where the use of small escalations of commitment will guide your way until we arrive at your destination (hopefully to kids and a yard with a white picket fence in this example). First, we ask for a commitment of time. Then, a commitment of personal information, a commitment of vulnerability, and finally something more like a sale.

So how do you escalate the commitment in a sales relationship?

A **"Lead magnet"** is often your businesses "first date" with the potential customer. The commitment of their contact information and permission to follow up in exchange for something they find valuable, a lead magnet is the first conversion tool for qualified prospects who are experiencing a *pain point* you can solve. Information-based lead magnets are effective: like articles, checklists, guides, reports, or things they can download instantly in a **".PDF"** format and start using to solve one small, tangible part of their pain. All businesses can deploy information based lead magnets.

Giving your customers a lead magnet worthy of their time – and email address – is vital. It's a key step in establishing a deep bond of trust with your prospects and future customers. It can also generate authority for you with your audience as you demonstrate – up front – how much you have to offer them (in exchange for their contact information and permission to follow up, of course). Ultimately, the process is simple: value for value. Provide your customers that now and they'll reward you with purchases soon enough.

Lead magnets live at the very beginning of the sales journey and serve as a tool to attract as many qualified leads as possible. You don't need any fancy software to get started deploying lead magnets in your sales process:

"I made this great checklist for writing a Yelp profile that will outperform everyone else in your area. If you give me your email address, I'll send it to you as soon as I'm in front of a computer..." It's that simple.

Example 1:

- <u>Business</u>: Gardening supplies and plant nutrients
- Lead Magnet: Article, "7 Expert Tips for Stubborn Orchids" ←
- <u>Analysis</u>: This company sells a proprietary blend of advanced orchid nutrients and supplies but has found that because Orchids are so hard to grow, gardeners with these flowers desperately need additional support if they want to have beautiful specimens. Their lead magnet "7 Expert Tips to Best Care for Stubborn Orchids," is perfect because only someone struggling with their orchids would be interested in such information and people who download have qualified themselves as strong potential customers

for what they sell.

Example 2:

- Business: HVAC
- Lead Magnet: Article, "The 5 Worst Indoor Air Pollutants" ←
- Analysis: This company sells heating, ventilation, and air conditioning products and services but their biggest money maker is their hypoallergenic air filters, often replacing them seasonally on systems they've installed over the years. This article is a great reminder for people that they may be due for their regular service. Anyone who downloads or views this guide will likely be more open to having a technician in their home to inspect their filters and ducts.

Example 3:

- Business: Life coaching
- Lead Magnet: Checklist, "7 Signs You Aren't Living Your Best Life" ←
- Analysis: Someone who is unsure or needing validation that they are or aren't living their best life are exactly the people who need support and guidance to keep them moving forward, making them a perfect fit for Life Coaching offers.

A percentage of people taking you up on your lead magnet are just there for something free and that's ok, we always want to be of service. The problem with that comes down the road when you as a marketer are spending actual time trying to nurture a sales relationship with these people who aren't qualified and have no intention of buying. We need an effective way to separate between them and your future customers and *loyals* so you know who is worthy of your precious sales energy.

It's been said that anyone who spends some money with you is 2000% more likely to spend more money with you as long as you delivered the right value. So, if we ask the people who request our *lead magnet* to spend a tiny amount upfront, those who take action are likely way more qualified to buy your primary offer than someone who doesn't.

This tool is a **"tripwire:"** a low price, high-value offer, often between $3-$9 depending on your business, that strongly encourages newly generated leads to get out their credit cards and make a commitment of actual dollars. This will tell you who is there to act and who isn't, right off the bat. Correctly positioned, the tripwire should be irresistible to the right qualified target and will, therefore, convert at a very high rate – but the trick is to over-deliver.

Example 1:

- Business: Gardening supplies and plant nutrients
- Lead Magnet: Article, "7 Expert Tips for Stubborn Orchids"
- **Tripwire**: $7 Guide, "14 Day Orchid Rehab" ←
- **Analysis**: Someone who needs a guide for rehabilitating their orchids absolutely also needs the right nutrients to make it happen, making them the perfect fit for this company's advanced supplement blends.

Example 2:

- Business: HVAC
- Lead Magnet: Article, "5 Worst Indoor Air Pollutants"
- **Tripwire**: Fan Filters ← (These $7-$11 products are made by the same companies as the premium air filters but are designed to slip on all home plug-in oscillating, box, and tower fans.)
- **Analysis**: Someone who is interested in buying a fan filter is very likely to be the perfect customer for their premium home air filters several times a year.

Example 3:

- Business: Life coaching
- Lead Magnet: Checklist, "7 Signs You Aren't Living Your Best Life"
- **Tripwire**: $9 access to The Digital Boot Camp On Stepping into Your Best You ←
- **Analysis**: This virtual webinar-style training has high perceived value and beyond being a great tripwire for people concerned with living a "better life," it will likely get high engagement; not only with fresh leads but also with warmer traffic who've bought offers recently and members of your top 20%. This webinar is a great opportunity to establish or reestablish loads of authority right before a big offer.

When you over deliver in your tripwire you cement your customers confidence in your authority to solve their larger problem and that makes them much more likely to purchase your *core offer*. But don't lose focus, your tripwire isn't about getting those few dollars, no. It's for separating your buyers from the looky loos, and it should be directly in line with the main thing you want them to buy.

<u>Primary offer:</u>" Also sometimes known as a **<u>core offer,</u>** this is the main thing you are focused on selling, the thing that this audience you're cultivating is most qualified to buy. Your primary offer will often be directly in line with the thing that you are in business to provide; If you are Nike, this is your Air-Jordan. If you are Coach, this is one of your clutch handbags. If you are Harley Davidson, this is an actual motorcycle.

The trip-wire should pre-qualify these leads beforehand and make your primary offer an easy close because they've already proven they are the right fit:

<u>Example 1:</u>

- <u>Business</u>: Gardening supplies and plant nutrients
- Lead Magnet: Article, "7 Expert Tips for Stubborn Orchids"
- Tripwire: $7 Guide, "14 Day Orchid Rehab"
- Primary Offer: $147 Ultimate Nutrient Mixes for Orchids(monthly) ←

<u>Analysis</u>: This offer gets to the heart of the pain their audience is in - their flowers are dying because they don't have the right tools. The lead magnet proved they had orchids and the *tripwire* confirmed they are struggling with them, so this primary offer of an actual nutrient mix for them to use on their orchids along with the training guide is congruent and works well together to solve a larger problem.

Example 2:

- Business: HVAC
- Lead Magnet: Article, "5 Worst Indoor Air Pollutants"
- Tripwire: $7-11 Fan Filters
- Primary Offer: Home inspection with $129.99 air filter replacement package as needed ←

Analysis: If the consumer has people in their homes or business suffering with things like asthma or allergies, air pollutants can be serious triggers for them. Someone who downloads an article to learn more about the worst indoor air pollutants have qualified themselves as being concerned with their air quality and buying a fan filter confirms it as a fact. This person has identified themselves as a great fit for an in-home air inspection offer and they are likely someone who would purchase hypoallergenic air filters not just once, but on a regular basis.

Example 3:

- Business: Life coaching
- Lead Magnet: Checklist, "7 Signs You Aren't Living Your Best Life"
- Tripwire: $9 access to The Digital Summit On Becoming Your Best You
- Primary Offer: $2499 "Best You" 3 month awakening program with in-person intensive experience ←

Analysis: It may be reasonable to suspect that an individual who requests a checklist to determine whether they're living their best lives, may be concerned that they aren't. If they then attend a digital summit on becoming their best selves, it confirms that they are looking for a solution to that feeling. A 3 month program is likely exactly the structure and support this type of person needs to reposition themselves and find more fulfillment.

All of these offers serve to qualify someone with a singular pain.

When your offer is aligned with your previous steps, your leads will be drawn through the funnel up to this point where they have made a primary purchase. Even though a little celebration is in order, first you want to make sure that you have given them every opportunity to let you improve their lives as encompassingly as possible; but that requires another step:

The **"Upsell:"** Ask them to buy something else on the way out. We know they're "in the store" and are in a buying mindset, so is there anything wrong with encouraging them to put something else in their cart? Maybe something that would make the experience with their first purchase even better? How about an extra layer of service?

Some business owners are reluctant to ask a customer to buy something else after they just made a purchase but consider this: even companies that just sold you a $65,000 car have no problem looking you right in the eye and asking if you want to take their special coverages and amenities and thousands of dollars more in extras. My tailor is always looking for ways to throw cufflinks and extra accouterments on my ticket. My corner convenience store asks me if I want a king-size PayDay bar every time I come in for gas, and guess what - now I buy one even if the new guy forgets to offer.

None of these things are bad. It's these businesses job to make sure you have absolutely everything you need. Some people want all the coverages and amenities. Some people need the extra pairs of socks and ties. Sometimes I just need a candy bar. If these businesses can pull it off, you can too, but it's all about understanding your audience relative to the pain you are solving. So what else can you add to their transaction to serve them better?

Maid services can add a refrigerator scrub or pantry refresh for some extra cash. A clothing business can suggest a belt purchase with every pants sale and cufflinks with every shirt. A coach can offer access to a popular webinar or training when a client purchases consulting.

> **"Upsell Protocol:' If someone purchases X, we offer them Y. Every sale, every time."**

The trick to a successful upsell is making sure you fully understand the problem you are solving with the previous purchase and that you're providing the right type of supplemental value for the next.

Most people may say no, but that doesn't matter. If you can get 20% of your new customers to make one more purchase with you every time, what would that actually look like on your bottom line?

80/20 Success Tip:

The customers who buy an upsell along with their original purchase will have a very high likelihood of being future loyal customers. Keep their contact info close and segment them in your list.

Implementing clear upsell protocol is a key pillar of **"sales packing,"** or maximizing your customers average spend per transaction, and a it's a surefire way to improve margins overall in one easy step. You really should have something else strategically positioned to offer customers right at the point of purchase for each of your products. That alone can put a respectable bump in your revenue with one simple additional action by the sales department.

Follow these steps to create the basics you need for mapping your automation blueprint top to bottom.

Imagine focusing your efforts on going out, meeting more people and qualifying new leads because you know exactly what's happening for every single one of them on the back end. You know they're being properly nurtured with a high touch sales campaign in place that will take them to the *choke point*; from *lead magnet*, to *trip wire*, to a core sale and an upsell.

No more writing fresh sales materials or emails on the fly for leads as they come in or feeling anxious over lost deals ever again. That's what's on the other side of this automation process, so don't get discouraged. Your business needs a solid sales plan, it's non-negotiable if you intend on breaking through to the next level.

Set up some really solid pieces that cover 80% of your *lead sources* and then just trust in the system you've built: with this outline firmly in place you can handle 10 or 100 or 1000 new leads confidently knowing that your business will turn a steady percentage of them into closed sales with less guesswork than before. That's a formula for sustainable growth.

You really can reach six figures or higher executing your map manually without automation software if you are diligent, but be warned: it takes discipline and religious levels of attention to maintain consistency and make sure nobody is getting lost. I highly recommend automation software for anyone ready to start having these nurture functions performed more efficiently. It will help you stay positive that none of your valuable leads are slipping through the cracks in the bustle of all the other things you are overseeing in your day to day as the *Chief Marketer.*

> **"Processes make the difference between a hustle and a business."**

Campaigns can be designed for each of your products and *lead sources* until you have a path for each new prospect and your business is completely and clearly laid out for any team member or software to follow. This is the foundation of successfully automating your sales system. But even with the best blueprint in the world you won't get far without the right language…

CHAPTER 11

CONTENT 101:
Marketing Linguistics

"You talkin' to me?" (Taxi Driver, 1976)

If you expect someone to understand you, it's really best if you speak the same language.

"Speaking their (your clients) language:" is the practice of incorporating the same words and phrases your customers are using to talk about the problem that you solve. More powerful than just traditional "mirroring" tactics, speaking your customers language builds trust, connects faster and shortens the sales cycle way more effectively than just saying "My company's name is ABC and I sell XYZ..."

I discovered this ideology the hard way through very expensive trial and error. Right after college I was launching my video marketing company and was having a rather difficult time doing it. I had the skills, credentials, equipment and testimonials to prove I could make profitable marketing **"content"** but I just always seemed to have the hardest time closing the sale, even in front of the perfect qualified lead.

I would meet great potential clients at networking events or online and we would really hit it off. They loved my work and we were connecting as people, talking about their business and everything else, but when I asked for the credit card to seal the deal I was running into a huge disconnect - they always needed to think about it or do some research first before pulling the trigger. The sales conversation always felt like an uphill battle and I just began thinking that was how things worked. Then one day when talking with the owner of a pizza chain at a conference in Phoenix, I saw it happening again but this time I was blessed with a breakthrough.

As I'm giving the owner my prices and began to move toward closing the sale, I started explaining that I would do all of the pre-production, script copywriting, offer crafting, location services, film the whole thing on my dual Blackmagic Digital Cinema Cameras in 4K and include the color grading, color correction, editing, dynamic text, platform integration, "blah blah blah..." As a recent graduate of film school, I was so proud of all of these things I could do and rattled them off like I'd done 500 times before, but then the prospect turned around and called to his partner who was on the other side of the room.

As he introduced me he said to his partner, "This is Ashley, he's a video marketing expert, he'll finally write us some great ads, shoot them, and do all the editing stuff for us. Yes, *"editing stuff."* It hurt a little to hear my years of training and expertise distilled into just two words, but his partner watched a video of mine on his phone and immediately agreed to work with me without hesitation. And in that moment I realized I'd been completely failing to speak my target's language the whole time.

Business owners and entrepreneurs don't care about color grading, they don't care about how fancy my camera is, they didn't even really care that I'd worked for the Discovery Channel, and me talking about all of it just confused and overwhelmed them. All they wanted to hear out of me was that A.) I could alleviate the pain they were suffering from not having professional video and B.) having to do it themselves. .

> *I was speaking a filmmakers language not the business owners language and it was costing me big every single day without even knowing it.*

From this point on I would meet people I wanted to work with and after we connected I would tell them exactly what they wanted to hear: "I'm a video expert, I write, shoot, and I'll do all the editing stuff on some really killer marketing videos for your company so you don't have to worry about it anymore…"

All of a sudden my sales game turned around and I went on to sign six figures in new contracts that year.

What is your "editing stuff?"

Is there something in your message that's turning your leads off or maybe just not connecting as well as it could? Think about the last few opportunities you lost: maybe it really wasn't the right time or the right fit for that person, but is it possible, just possible, that you were speaking the wrong language?

Carefully listen to the exact words your customers and potential customers use when talking about the problem that you solve from now on, because once you pick up their vocabulary it becomes much easier for you to communicate in ways that cut through the noise and lead to more sales with less selling.

Once you've found what those words and phrases are, I highly encourage you to have them clearly visible in your *brand bible* for reference later to keep you or your marketing team focused and on track as you grow and create more *content*.

The message is what you say, but how you say it can be just as influential. Two sales ingredients should be heavily incorporated into every single interaction your prospect or customer has with your brand:

PASSION + GRATITUDE = CHARISMA

People want to work with experts who are passionate about what they do. The only thing more contagious than enthusiasm is a lack of enthusiasm and the fact is that nobody will ever be as excited about your business as you are. That makes it your responsibility as the marketer to bring the right energy to the table whether you are composing an email, a blog, in person or on a phone call. What you do matters and you are grateful you get to do it for people like them.

Gratitude is necessary. No matter how you look at it, someone could be doing something other than paying attention to you. Reminding someone that you value their presence will go a long way to starting every interaction on the right note. But that won't be enough if you can't confidently solve their problem.

CONTENT 101: Marketing Linguistics

"The pain point is the paying point"

Use this mantra to create all of the sales and marketing you do from here on. It's a universal fact whether you are online or face to face: *People don't make buying decisions from a place of pleasure, they do it to escape some type of pain.*

You need to know what hurts and how to make it better. If you can locate your customers main **"pain points"** and address it directly using their own words, you will have much better chances of getting them to **"self-select,"** which is the phenomenon where a message resonates so strongly with someone that they seek you out to help them instead of the other way around. This occurs when someone sees you as the perfect fit and is by far the best form of sales conversion because it requires little to no back and forth to manifest the purchase.

One of the first places I like to start when creating sales material for a client is right where their future customer is in pain at this moment. What does that feel like? How does that affect them every day? For some businesses the pain point that they solve is visceral and will directly influence everything and everyone in their life - use that. If you can distill your solution to these basic human universal elements your words will resonate directly to the core of the place in people's brain that drives them to buy:

- An acupuncture business doesn't just provide acupuncture - it gives relief to the man suffering because he can't play with his child due to chronic pain and it's affecting their relationship during important years he'll never get back. That person is in pain, isolated, worried and depressed that they aren't being a better father and husband.

- A security company doesn't just sell homeowners their security systems - it lets a working professional mom feel more comfortable going on long business trips knowing that her loved ones and livelihood at home are safe and secure. That person is preoccupied worrying if their family is safe in a neighborhood where things may not be as calm as they'd like and it is affecting their focus on their career.
- A clothing company doesn't just sell garments - it helps those in their tribe express themselves to the world through fashion and styles they might not have access to otherwise due to their size, culture, or ethnicity. As a curator of a particular collection, they really help their customers be their most authentic self. This individual is feeling stifled and unheard or may be constantly overlooked in the office and the right outfit could be what it takes to finally be their best.

Every single business is more than the thing they make or do, they are solving a real and painful problem for their customers that should improve their lives in big ways, no matter the industry. That means you'll need to be clear on exactly what that is so you can use it to your advantage and it absolutely needs to be the basis of your message.

But if you want to grow and scale you will have to be able to connect not just face to face but through the words on your website, in your *messaging*, and throughout your sales process.

How do you use your new language skills to create written *content* that will captivate and connect with your audience?

CHAPTER 12

CONTENT 201:
Copywriting & the P.S.P.S. Model

"Wax on, wax off. Wax on, Wax off"
(The Karate Kid, 1984)

A successful marketer is a strategist, an artist and a psychologist all at the same time - nowhere more so than when writing copy for their business.

What you say and how you say it may actually influence your target more than the quality of your product or service itself, at least initially. **"Copy"** is the marketing term we use to describe a specific combination of words you'll choose when writing for your business.

Words in advertisements are copy. Slogans are copy. Text on your website is copy. Scripts are copy. The language in your emails, offers, and letters is considered copy. If it is written by your company to be received by your customers, potential customers, sponsors, affiliates or partners with the intention of persuading them to do something, it is "copy."

Marketers use this term to give sales words the extra importance they deserve due to how each one you choose can influence your audiences behavior so much.

> **FACT:** *"Butt-dialing" someone and "Booty-calling" them are completely different things even though they are essentially synonyms.*

Words have power both directly and indirectly; the tones, tenses, and exact language you choose tells your audience everything about your brand. Are you formal or casual? Do you use big words or slang? Contemporary or traditional? Your vocabulary will influence how someone interprets what you're saying and inform them whether or not you connect on the right levels to buy.

Even businesses with tremendous potential can be stifled by an inability to hit a nerve with their audience and then struggle to figure out why - it's often in the copy.

Either the hardest or easiest part of the marketing process depending on who you ask, good copywriting isn't about creativity, although a little certainly doesn't hurt. It's a mix between art and science. A dance between connection and persuasion. But what makes copy so critical to your sales process?

If your business had an actual audible voice that your customers could hear it would *sound* like your copy.

So ask yourself, is it hip? Is it serious? Is it inspirational? Masculine or feminine? Playful, adventurous, flirty, or bold?

This is your **tone:** a feeling or vibe that your company gives off through a combination of your words, phrases, position, and presentation. It's how your company *feels* to your audience and you need to know that if you're currently in business, you've probably already cultivated one whether it's intentional or not. Evaluate your web presence, social media, emails, videos, and branding. Are you giving off the right tone when you communicate?

It's important to know that good creative writing and good sales copy are two completely different ballparks. They're not even the same sport.

Copywriting isn't about dressing up the message, impressing anyone, or being witty, and if you find yourself trying to accomplish any of those things it can actually land you in trouble. Everything you write should be consciously about driving an action. Period. It serves all other purposes second. If you are writing anything on the sales side for your business from this point on, always ask yourself this: "what do I want the reader to do immediately?" If it isn't crystal clear in the copy it probably needs to be sent back for another attempt.

This ask or **"CALL TO ACTION (C.T.A.),."** is a place, often near the end of your email, article, text, video or piece of *content* where you tell someone exactly what you want them to do and how: *Click this button. Schedule time on my calendar here. Show up tomorrow at noon. Join my Facebook group. Buy now. Email me back. Post a testimonial on social media. Use this hashtag.*

Anything you are specifically asking the person to do in

your *copy* is the *C.T.A.* and almost everything you write for your business should have one. Every single piece of *content* you are planning should have a purpose: either to *initiate*, *engage*, or otherwise get the right people to their respective *choke point* quickly.

Content and copy are two different things. As where copy is the actual words or phrases used in writing for your business, **"content"** is the term used to describe the actual piece itself. An article is *content* and is made of words that are copy. My social media post is *content*, the title and words are copy. My lead capture page is *content*, the words on it are the copy.

Lots of business owners who are handling their own copywriting for the first time will struggle to get started but will find their footing with practice so don't be afraid to try even if you find it uncomfortable in the beginning. As the *Chief Marketer*, challenge yourself to complete a project or assignment in a certain amount of time several times a week. Your first attempt might be rough, but your 50th will be much better. You'll be there faster than you think if you are diligent - just don't give up.

Different people will approach the creative process in their own way, but I've found that coming up with good *content* and copy is far easier in a room with smart people you like, where you can get honest feedback in a supportive environment. But when collaborating with other people it's important to maintain a positive energy without criticism. I always tell the teams I'm working with that there are no wrong answers in the *writers-room*:

A **"writers-room"** is any place where certain trusted, qualified people have the opportunity to contribute or give feedback on things like your copy or creative *content* direction. Just like I believe that great marketing is a team sport, copywriting is best when you can get more than one perspective on the final product. But it's also important to make sure that you aren't getting input from the wrong people. Family members and friends can be poor resources for constructive feedback unless they are initiated to your brand or business in general. There are times when you just need an honest gut reaction to something but most of the time it is important to choose who you rely on to influence your *content* wisely.

6 Expert Shortcuts For Writing Strong Copy:

1. Begin with the end in mind: Knowing the purpose of the content you're creating and where it fits in the sales cycle or blueprint will help you get your target from point A to Point B efficiently.

2. Be clear: Make sure you aren't adding any unnecessary steps between your message and the choke point. Always ask yourself if someone consuming your content can follow you directly to what you are asking in the *C.T.A.* and get there without distraction.

3. Present the *C.T.A.* as the feature: Not the other way around. If you can be excited about what you want someone to do, it's much easier to write content to support it. Remember, the readers lives will be better once they take you up on your offer; if not you need

to revisit your positioning.

4. Check for redundant words: These can be distracting for readers that notice them and are generally easy to prevent with a quick trip to your favorite thesaurus.

5. Proof read it out loud: You will catch errors easier when you are speaking audibly - no audience required. I often read copy out loud to myself in an empty room. They can call me crazy, but they can't call me a bad writer.

6. Collaborate: Find your writers-room. This communal experience is good for all parts of the marketing and creative process. That special person's perspective can change everything.

Even professional copywriters will sometimes need multiple drafts before finding exactly how to make something as persuasive as possible. Don't worry, it gets easier as more *content* is created and your business finds its unique voice.

Although there's more to learn about writing for all of the specific platforms like email, blogs, text, web pages and everything else you may need the most powerful fundamentals of copywriting are universal and rooted in the *problem solution problem solution model...*

"P.S.P.S. (Problem-Solution-Problem-Solution) MODEL:"

An incredibly versatile rinse and repeat process that directly leverages pain into action using cause and effect.

Although you might be better off thinking of it as **<u>trust marketing.</u>** P.S.P.S. logic should be the backbone that supports all of the *content* you're creating for your business. It's the smoothest and most effective way to gently walk qualified prospects through the sales journey step by step without being pushy or investing a ton of time sorting out every lead.

<u>The secret ingredient is value:</u> You have to make their lives at least a little better with every step.

The idea is simple: first identify a common pain point that your target audience has, then find a way to show them how to solve it. Not all of it, but just one small, manageable part of it - enough to earn their trust. Then use that trust to get them to take a another step and then another and another.

Step 1: Your Title is a Promise

Your audience wants to know what they are getting up front. Whenever you are sharing valuable *content* or information, promise what they are going to get for their commitment in the title. You must be able to fulfill your promise by the end of the interaction so be very specific about what they will walk away with.

Examples of titles:

Bad: 3 Steps to Grow Your Business
Good: 3 Steps For More Yelp Reviews in 7 day

Bad: 3 tips for dressing better
Good: 3 tips for standing out in the office this spring

Bad: 3 tools for a better team
Good: 3 tools for more successful team meetings

Notice how all of the bad examples are broad and almost impossible to completely tackle in one sitting. If we want the *P.S.P.S. model* to work, by the end of the *content* we need our audience member to have one clear solution and say "Wow, what's next?"

Once you've delivered on the *Promise of the Premise*, you can do what you say you can, the *P.S.P.S. model* dictates that you show them the next challenge they are going to face and they will naturally trust that you are the perfect one to solve that too. Now you are operating a **"funnel."**

The **"Promise of the Premise"** is another term from the filmmaking world that lends itself very well to the science of marketing.

When most of us pay to see a movie, it's fair to say that

CONTENT 201: Copywriting & the P.S.P.S. Model

we generally know what we're about to be in for. Just like in business, there is a social contract between the company (the filmmaker) and the customer (the audience goer) that they will deliver on what is expected. If you see posters and trailers and specials on late night shows for a movie highlighting two lovers getting married or maybe some light romantic comedy you might buy tickets for you and your special someone on Friday night. But if you get to the theater and find 20 minutes in that you've walked into something a lot more like the *Texas Chainsaw Massacre*, you'd have every reason to be upset. Trust would be broken. You might not see something from that director or production company ever again.

On the other hand, if the director delivers on the romantic rendezvous of a lifetime and your date goes "extra well," you're going to be way more likely to see something else advertised as "directed by the people who brought you that first thing you liked."

This happens all the time in marketing. A business will promise to solve one problem or deliver some type of specific value but either can't quite pull it off, address something slightly off topic or another thing entirely. When that happens they lose trust and therefore leads and therefore money.

Be careful that when using the *P.S.P.S. model* to create content that you are clearly delivering on exactly what you promised. Bonus points if you can make it sexy for your target.

Remember, nobody wants homework. I try to keep the number of steps in my content below 7 so that we don't lose people who are busy or have short attention spans.

If you have one amazing, powerful, game-changing point then you should absolutely choose a title more like *"The Number One Thing I Wish I Had Known Before XYZ,"* there's nothing wrong with going that direction but be warned, it better be good.

With your offer positioned behind the right problem, next it's tome to structure our solution properly and in the right order.

Step 2: Organize the Content

Organizing the body of your *P.S.P.S. content* can be as easy as 1, 2, 3.

1. **Lead with your best point** - This hooks the reader in to stay until the *C.T.A.* *Include steps that the target can follow to get a result - This encourages the reader to follow along.

2. **Set up the next problem** - This smoothly gets them to transition toward the *choke point*.

3. **Be brief** - Remember your copywriting fundamentals: speak your customers language and be concise when you write.

This is all you need to begin proving your authority and earning their trust.

Step 3: Embed the *C.T.A.*

Your last point should be your call to action, not in a pitch after your last point. We want the real *C.T.A.* to be triggered subliminally before we offer anything...

Examples of *P.S.P.S. Content*:

Business A: *Financial planning*
5 Money Moves for a Comfortable Retirement in Southern California:

1. Forget traditional 401Ks
2. Invest in hard assets like real estate
3. Stay current on activity and risk
4. Have a realistic savings plan
5. Find an advisor you can trust. → C.T.A.

Subliminal *C.T.A.*: Now that I know how to plan for retirement, I need the right advisor I can trust.

Business B: *Workout Supplements*
5 Keys to Better Protein Digestion & Bigger Muscles

1. Drink 2 glasses of water immediately when you wake up and again at noon.
2. Eat less than 750 calories per sitting, frequently.
3. Stay away from spicy foods and smoking.
4. Don't fall for knockoff whey proteins
5. Incorporate certified Digestive Enzymes → *C.T.A.*

Subliminal *C.T.A.*: Now that I know how to digest more of my protein for bigger muscles, I need to know how I can make it even better with these certified digestive enzymes.

Business C: *Executive coaching*
5 Top Killers of CEO's Productivity
1. Not having the result in mind
2. "Nesting" or being comfortable
3. Not having a schedule
4. Not having a system in place
5. No Professional Accountability → C.T.A.

Subliminal *C.T.A.*: Now that I know how to tackle the biggest killers of my productivity, I need the right coach to keep me accountable.

In all of these examples, the *C.T.A.* is hidden in the last point, opening up the conversation of how you can step in and help them. Understand this and unlock the magic behind never having to be salesy ever again - it will change your life as a business owner and marketer.

Step 4: The Opportunity

The *P.S.P.S. model* is designed to smoothly escalate the commitment between you and your target. Someone sitting down to listen to you is a commitment of their time. Them opting in for valuable content is a commitment of their personal information. Them buying from you is a commitment of their hard earned money. All of these commitments require trust and the *P.S.P.S. model* is all about stacking trust very efficiently, very quickly.

With the subliminal *C.T.A.*, in place, your next step is as simple as gently placing the next solution near the target. You shouldn't even have to make a direct pitch, they'll just be drawn to it:

CONTENT 201: Copywriting & the P.S.P.S. Model

Business A: *Financial Planning*

- 5 Money Moves for a Comfortable Retirement in Southern California:
- Subliminal C.T.A.: "Now that I know how to plan for retirement, I need the right advisor I can trust."
- The Opportunity: ←
- <u>"Thanks for listening today! Lots of people have more questions on putting these steps in place for themselves or a loved one, If that's you don't worry - just stop by my booth for a spot on my calendar."</u>

Business B: *Workout Supplements*

- 5 Keys to Better Protein Digestion & Bigger Muscles
- Subliminal C.T.A.: "Now that I know how to digest more of my protein for bigger muscles, I need to know how I can get these certified digestive enzymes."
- The Opportunity: ←
- <u>"Thank you so much for being a member of our community and reading my article! If you want to learn more about the best proteins for mass or maybe even check out some of our certified digestive enzymes, I'm putting a link and a promo code below."</u>

Cont.

Business C: *Executive coaching*

- 5 Top Killers of CEO's Productivity
- Subliminal C.T.A.: "Now that I know how to tackle the biggest killers of my productivity, I need the right coach to keep me accountable."
- The Opportunity: ←
- <u>"I'm beyond grateful you watched this video! To say thank you for spending your very valuable time with me I'm giving you access to my "7-day Accountability Challenge" - just put down $1 so I know you're serious about making it happen and you can get started."</u>

Practice using the *P.S.P.S. model* in your emails, blogs, articles, Facebook posts, stage talks, and more. When speaking the right language combined with the *P.S.P.S. model* and *H.T.C.M.*, you have all of the makings you need for clear, profitable communication. You're one step closer to becoming a persuasive marketer, but you have to be hungry for what comes next...

CHAPTER 13

SALES 201:
Delicious Offers & Promotions

"I'm going to make him an offer he can't refuse"
(The Godfather, 1972)

The word *offer* can be confused for a few different things so it's important to clarify what we mean for this context: beyond just a proposition to buy something, an **<u>offer</u>** is your products or services positioned in a way that increases the perception of overall value. Done correctly they should increase the attractiveness to the target.

More than just a product alone, offers are a package of value with particular stipulations attached and you'll need to know how to use them reliably to drive consistent revenue. There's a reason why you see them everywhere you look:

- Get this years Honda Accord at under 3% APR for the Holiday Sign and Drive Event - Ends Jan 1st.
- Buy the three for $3 deal and get three for the price of one - during happy hour between 6-8pm all summer.
- Get this package and we'll throw in a bonus hour of one-on-one support - for new members who buy today.
- Try my coaching program for 7 days, just put $1 down! Only if you sign up in the next 30 minutes.

All of these are respectable examples of a business positioning the deal from a certain angle to *engage* someone who may be otherwise on the fence. This is important for generating consistent action when content alone might not be enough. Sometimes we have educated and **"initiated"** perfectly but the target is simply waiting for the *right time to buy*. A strategic offer will pick those low hanging fruit before they **"rot,"** or expire because there's nothing more maddening than losing a deal you already had in the bag:

Several years ago I attended an automation conference in a big city a few hours away from where I was living at the time. While there I met lots of great prospects but one person stood out as the perfect client - a true whale. He owned a big gym in Washington D.C. and had flown in to learn about automating his sales and membership processes. As an automation expert and due to the fact that I'd managed the largest boxing club in the Southwest not long before that, we had tons to talk about.

I spent more time with him than the other leads at the event because I was so sure he was going to take me up on a full automation rebuild and by the end of the three days he'd essentially told me as much although I never made him an actual offer.

Conferences like the one we were at can be very exhausting, it was getting late, and I was in a hurry to get the drive back home over. He and I shared our information, set a time to get the paperwork signed and everything the next morning and exchanged a big hug. On the drive home I was on the phone with my partner when I received a call from a DC area code. I assumed this might be him but since we had a conversation scheduled at 9 the next morning and being that I was only 30 minutes to the house I let it go to voicemail. As soon as I put my bags down I gave him a text back, no answer. Then a call, no answer. Then he's late for our morning call the next day, and after blowing up his phone over and over, I get a text back explaining that while waiting for his Uber to the airport he was standing next to who turned out to be the owner of a rival automation company and the guy had made my lead an offer he couldn't refuse... The worst part was weeks later when I found out he paid them way more than he would have if he'd gone with me and they didn't even have the fitness industry experience I did.

That's the power of having the right offer with the right value in front of the right person right when they need it. Someone may say "yes" in the moment if it will solve their pain.

Learn from my mistake: time is not your friend and deals will *rot* if you let them. When a prospect thinks you may be the right fit, you have to get them to make a commitment before they change their mind or find a solution somewhere else. Often enough, an offer is the perfect tool for making sure that doesn't happen but it has to be something they can't resist. It has to make their mouth water.

> **A "Delicious Offer" has three main ingredients:**
>
> 1. **Special Value:** The customer will get something they really want but with increased value.
> 2. **Reason:** "We don't normally do this but due to special circumstances…"
> 3. **Limitation:** Urgency encourages action.

- **1. Special Value:** Sometimes the key product is enough and all the consumer is looking for is a reason to buy. For these people it can be appropriate to add additional value in one of two ways:
- Discounts: Personally I avoid coupons or discounts but sometimes they are the right answer for the circumstance. When given the opportunity, I would rather add value than reduce price. Before committing to a coupon, try brainstorming something you can add that doesn't cost you anything to deliver but will still increase the perceived value of the purchase and allow you to retain the full revenue - look to information based value-adds or bonuses.
- Bonuses: Throwing in something else. Bonuses increase value by putting an extra product or service in someones hand when they check out. Not to be confused with an upsell, bonuses come with no observable increase in price. I always try to find bonuses that don't require a physical deliverable or a one-on-one commitment of time. Self study programs, downloads, workshops, and video or group trainings are great choices for a bonus and can even drive more sales down the line.

2. Reason: This is where business owners and marketers most often get stumped and the behind-the-scenes-truth is that it's likely the least important part of your irresistible offer if you have provided enough value. The reason for your special offer is just a great excuse to include fun imagery and language that may further excite your audience.

- Holidays: a great place to start planning an offer. New Years, Easter, Fourth of July, Thanksgiving, Halloween, any of "the Day's" (Presidents, Veterans, Valentines, Mothers, etc.), it doesn't matter as long as it's cohesive with your brand and works for who you serve.
- Seasonal Specials: Spring-flings, Summer-slams, a Fall blowout, Winter gift specials. That's four great offers to run every year. Name them as you see fit but don't overthink the classics.
- **"VIP" Offers**: sometimes people deserve a special deal based on their previous actions; that's when to deploy a VIP offer. Has it been one year since they joined your list? "Here's something special on me with your next purchase!" "It's nice to meet you, here's an introductory offer." Sometimes the target doesn't even need to know they are getting a VIP offer at all and just all of a sudden receive something great that's just right for them based on their activity.

Everyone is different, but there are some universal milestones in your business that may be worth celebrating. Make a list or add this information to your database so that you know when it's time to use these.

Then there are offers triggered by **"revenue thresholds."**

Someone who spends $100,000 may get a special invitation for a VIP training retreat at a vacation destination for an irresistible price including airfare, but of course this cost is already calculated into the lifetime *R.O.I.*, so although not everyone could get this offer - it's just right for these *loyals* or *whales* who may spend another $100,000 in the next six months.

There are tons of great ways to use VIP offers, especially if you are willing to track behavior over time.

Cultural & Regional Celebrations: can be particularly useful if handled with savvy. Do you sell somewhere like Boston with a large Irish influence? A St. Patrick's Day promotion can be wildly successful in almost any industry. Do you do business in the Southwest? Consider a Cinco De Mayo offer. Serve a largely Jewish community? What do you have for Rosh Hashanah? You see this all the time with big businesses and may not even give it a second thought, but they're there because they really work and I look forward to Lent every year for the fish specials at my favorite restaurants.

Special Occasions: these are where I go when I feel like getting creative. Anything can be a special occasion and it can be really fun to come up with interesting reasons to deploy a special offer.

Record heat wave across the country? Did your business celebrate three years in its current location? Is a comet flying by? Did your state university win the big game? Let's celebrate together with a great deal! Any communal experience will do.

The pizza parlor by my house as a kid once had a special pizza offer for the manager's dog's birthday and that always stuck with me. When it's a special occasion you call the shots. Celebrate what you want when you want with your customers through a special promotion for something fun or unusual and let your companies personality shine. So, whens your dog's birthday?

3. Limitation: the limitation is critical because it tells the target how to respond to the offer. If they have 30 days to think about it, they may wait even if otherwise ready to buy. Other times a prospect may have 30 minutes to download their ticket or something to that effect. You even hear this on television advertisements where the narrator will say something similar to "if you call in the next 15 minutes..."

We don't actually believe that if we call 20 minutes from now they wouldn't honor the offer, maybe, but by setting that limitation they have informed the person considering the purchase how to respond - you have minutes to act.

The limitation must be tied to the value of the package, the reason for the offer, and where this product fits in your sales journey.

If this offer is at the beginning of the sales journey, the commitment may only be their email address or a few dollars; in this case you may only give them hours or days before the offer expires. If we are talking about something that is thousands and thousands of dollars or more, it may be appropriate to give someone days or weeks, possibly longer depending on the purchase and how much diligence is needed to make a responsible decision. We never want to be pushy or aggressive but as the experts it's important we get them what they really need.

Offers are special by definition because they are limited

in some way, if not they are a package or product but be warned, if you put an unreasonable limitation on your offer you will turn people off.

Here are some examples of commonly used *limitations:*

- **While Supplies Last:** "We only have so many at this price. We only have so many in stock. We only have so much time on our calendar. We only have 5 seats left."
- **For a Limited Time:** Until the end of the hour, day, week, month, season, or any other limited period of time.
- **Until XYZ:** Until our team is out of the playoffs, until the sub-freezing temperatures stop, until the groundhog sees his shadow.

With a strategic pitch in front of the right targeted leads, you're going to absolutely start seeing results on your weekly revenue numbers; congratulations. But now, armed with your list and a delicious offer, let's go adventuring into the world of sales.

"Bonus Lesson"

THE HISTORY OF MARKETING:
An Arms Race

"Resistance is Futile" (Star Trek: First Contact, 1996)

Although the role of the marketer has remained largely the same for generations, the tools and tactics we use have never stopped evolving.

New technologies have and will continue to play an unmistakable role in how businesses like yours reach and engage more people, just as they have for hundreds of year.

Those who embraced these ever changing technologies found wild success, while those who resisted rarely recovered. Technology is not the enemy:

(The Pre-Modern Age)

1439 – Johannes Gutenberg develops the movable type printing press in Europe (Bi Sheng accomplished the same in China between 1041 and 1048).

-A communication revolution follows: for the first time, someone could reliably mass-communicate with others hundreds of miles away without leaving home.

1480 – William Caxton debuts first printed advertisement for books, it quickly becomes standard practice. A boon follows.

1605 – Johan Carolus publishes the first modern newspaper, bringing both updates and editorials into peoples homes on a regular basis.

1730s – Magazines emerge as popular media, putting topic specific or *niche* content into many peoples hands for the first time.

1741 – Benjamin Franklin publishes the Pennsylvania Gazette, making it the second magazine in the Americas after Andrew Bradford publishes *The American* three days prior.

1743 – Franklin introduces graphic art into his advertisement because he notices they catch the readers eye better. It works brilliantly and the practice quickly becomes industry standard.

THE HISTORY OF MARKETING: An Arms Race

<u>1835</u> – The first billboard is erected in New York City by Jared Bell to advertise the circus, changing the relationship between businesses and their audiences forever...

From then on, people expect to be entertained.

<u>1836</u> – *La Presse* newspaper in Paris is the first to adopt paid advertising as part of it's business model to reduce the price to the consumer. It worked, and its success has been replicated ever since.

<u>1870s</u> – Posters take over: the more beautiful or striking, the better. First in Paris and then throughout the planet, posters become a disruptive mass medium for the communication of commerce and ideas.

-This is regarded as the birth of modern advertising.

<u>*(The Modern Age)*</u>

<u>1886</u> – The Yellow Pages are invented when a printer runs out of their standard inks, quickly becoming a primary source of traffic for businesses all across America.

<u>1922</u> – Radio begins broadcasting. Radio advertising immediately follows, infusing businesses into peoples homes and daily lives like never before.

<u>1941</u> – First TV advertisement is aired before a Dodgers baseball game by the Bulova Watch Company.

-TV surpasses magazine and radio advertising revenue combined in 1954.

1970 – Telemarketing, the ultimate in outbound marketing, begins in earnest, making companies millions on an unsuspecting public.

(The Digital Age)

1994 – The first pop-up banner appears on HotWired.com, with the text: "have you ever clicked your mouse right here?" "You will." A digital marketing culture begins.

1994 – An Arizona law firm posted an ad message on thousands of online newsgroups. *SPAM* is born.

1997 – Search engines emerge and with them the need for search engine optimization, several industries are born through this evolution.

-First Yahoo and Alta Vista In 1997, then Ask.com. Google and msn go live in 1998.

2003 – The CAN-SPAM Act is introduced. It features several measures designed to control *SPAM*.

2003 – The rise of social media begins with the founding of MySpace. LinkedIn and Facebook both are founded a year later.

2004 – Telemarketing changes forever with the start of the "Do Not Call" list.

2005 – Google introduces personalized search results, revolutionizing online advertising and putting more of the right products in front of the right people, driving ecommerce dollars by the millions.

2007 – 3G mobile networks let customers stream music and videos anywhere at an accelerated rate. Advertising in streaming platforms quickly becomes big business.

2012 – Over 40% of customers using inbound marketing techniques acquire a customer. Businesses plan to increase social media spending by 64%.

2016 – Mobile web browsing surpasses desktop usage for the first time at 51.3% and continues to grow with no end in sight.

It's now more important to have a mobile friendly site than a beautiful traditional site.

CHAPTER 14

SALES 301:
Email & T.O.M.

"These go to eleven" (This is Spinal Tap, 1984)

Email is the noble steed of your business. It provides a range of functions from communication, fulfillment, scheduling, reminding, outreach, nurture and more every day, but for our purposes here we're going to be talking about using it specifically in respect to sales and marketing.

"**Email marketing**" can be classified as either *target* or *broadcast marketing* depending on the strategy behind how it's employed and yes, it works. Email marketing is still incredibly profitable in the right hands, but it's largely dependent on the quality of the list you have put together and what language and *content* you choose. As the platform matures, audiences have become increasingly aware of sales pitches and it's more important than ever to lead with the right value and not be *salesy*. That makes the use of the *Problem Solution Problem Solution Model* and *High Touch Conversational Marketing Method* so incredibly effective here more than almost anywhere else.

The customer has very little tolerance for things that provide them no value and consumers consider nearly 80% of email to be SPAM. That means you'll need to be very strategic about what you send out.

"**SPAM**" is generally understood to be digital junk mail but it's a pretty broad term that's worth some definition. There is the SPAM that everyone would agree is unsolicited like the junk from strangers trying to increase the size of your endowment or begging you to help them get their inheritance out of Nigeria, but then there are companies you agreed to get stuff from that are sending out things you aren't interested in way too often.

For this second group, consumer email service providers like Gmail, Outlook, Yahoo and others have created things like *SPAM* and Promotion folders for the respective "junk" *content* but don't be fooled, both are to be avoided at all cost. As far as I know, nobody has ever opened one of these boxes on purpose so you don't want your emails hanging out there.

Outside of the qualification of whether your email was delivered to the real *inbox* or one of these impostor boxes, the term SPAM is relative and depends entirely on you the marketer. If someone gives you their email address for more information about solving a problem and you deliver on that it's "*nurture,*" but if you just send a newsletter or stuff that isn't valuable it's SPAM.

There are over 200 million online shoppers in the US

and 1.3 billion worldwide and they are only going to increase with time. An entire generation has now come of age only knowing a digital world. They not only prefer target marketing, they demand it, nowhere more so than in their email inbox.

The email landscape is changing but that's nothing to be afraid of. As the trash marketers out there fall by the wayside, the businesses that lead with value, cultivate, and engage real audiences of fans will succeed in far bigger ways than those who don't. But you need to know the facts of email marketing and that starts with an email's individual pieces:

Anatomy of an Email:

A. **From Field:** Ashley W. Webber (title@domain.com)
B. **Subject line:** Hey!
C. **Preview Window/Greeting Zone:** Troy! It's Ashley from The Book on Sales & Marketing.
D. **Email Body:** I had a great time checking out your facility last week. We got some really great stuff accomplished.

   I just wanted to check in and see how you're navigating the new auto-pilot system so far? ;)
E. **Primary C.T.A.:** If you're free, you should come to my *Conversion Boot Camp* downtown on the 22nd - just *register here* and I'll save you a seat.
F. **Salutation:** Keep it up,
G. **Signature:** Ashley Wilkes Webber
H. **P.S.:** I noticed we weren't connected on Facebook yet, what's up with that? Lol. Here's my page: (*Link*)

- **A. "From Field:"** Who does the email look like it's coming from? This is a factor that marketers and business owners forget can be changed. Often we want emails to look like they're coming from either us personally or from the company proper, but there are other options that can have a huge impact on the success of an email. At an event sponsorship I ran for a client we had a raffle *booth* where the first follow up email the entrants got came from the NAME OF COMPANY. That email had a tremendously lower open rate than the exact same email when sent from "NAME OF COMPANY *Prize Department*," even with the same subject line and even if it clearly said they didn't win in the *preview window*.
- **B. "Subject Line:"** This is where people expect you to indicate the specific reason for your email but you probably already know this can be used to generate excitement or mystery intended to influence the recipient into actually opening the email. The purpose of the subject line is solely to get a higher open rate.

Don't overlook the power of your subject lines or else you risk having a low open rate and thus fewer people reading your message - even if you have concocted the most valuable email in the world. You should know that sometimes I give myself hours to consider the best options for a subject line depending on who it's to and what I want them to do; words matter. The subject line is the first major thing most people notice after who the email is from so try to make it something that *stops them in their scrolling tracks*.

Try writing a subject line that reads as much like something you wrote to them personally one-on-one as possible instead of using clever setups or punchy references which will imply it's a general broadcast. Never forget the most successful marketing email of all time… a fundraising ask for President Obama's re-election campaign with a subject line of only 3 letters: "hey"

- **C. "Preview Window:"** Find this window inside your email feed directly after the end of the subject line. After the bold subject line, the preview window shows you the first 100 or so characters of the email before you open it. If you look through your email feed on your phone you'll likely find that most of the emails you get will begin with a variation of a simple greeting like "Hi, *YOUR NAME*." But some professional email service providers will allow you to adjust this window to reflect something other than what is actually at the beginning of the email to increase action. You can manipulate this window using consumer email providers like Gmail by writing what you want to be displayed in the preview window above the beginning of your actual email and then changing the font color to white - this is **"ghost text."**
- **C. "Greeting Zone:"** The very top of the email upon opening. Many businesses choose to include banners or logos in his area right above your introduction to the body of your email but it's not necessary, especially if you want the email to look more like it came from your personal account instead of a marketing system. Remember that not every email needs to start with "Hi, CONTACTS NAME." Mix it up every once in awhile, try starting with a question or a fact and then greet your recipient.
- **D. "Email Body:"** This is where you do most of your persuasion. The body of your text can be short or long.

Conversational or a "**Long Form Sales Format.**" It can include images, downloads, or even video but it all needs to be driving toward your Primary C.T.A..

- **E. "Primary C.T.A.:"** What is the purpose of this email? What would you like them to do? Everything you've planned up to this point should be in service of your primary C.T.A. Include the specific action you would like them to take, the timeframe for doing so, and clear instructions for committing to it.

- **F. "Salutation:"** The word, words, or phrase you use before you sign off of your email "Love, *Your Name*." "Best wishes, *Your Name*." "Hugs, *Your Name*." A consistent salutation or theme helps keep the voice familiar over multiple emails.

- **G. "Signature:"** How you identify yourself in the email tells the reader a lot about you, your authority and tone.

Be aware that "signature blocks"or preconstructed signature templates inside softwares like Infusionsoft or AWeber can be used by consumer email providers like GMail to tell between marketing and personal correspondence so stay out of the SPAM box and write your signature by hand.

- **H. "P.S.:"** The second most influential part of your email, the "*P.S.*" or *Postscript* comes after your signature and is traditionally read as an afterthought to the message itself but as you can probably guess we are going to be using it for sales instead.

Many readers will open an email and then jump directly to the bottom to see how long it is before going back up to the beginning to read your text body in full if everything checks out - that makes your P.S. line the second most trafficked part of the email after the subject line.

Some people use their *P.S.* for functional purposes like letting their readers know that they'll be out of the office or that their company will be updating their terms of agreement, and for corporate types that's fine, but as a marketer every *P.S.* should be a *C.T.A.* to get readers to a next best sales step. Either restate your primary *C.T.A.* or add another like "book time on my calendar *here*" or "take a look at this blog post I just wrote *here*." Doubling down on your original primary in the *C.T.A.* may capture some of the people who may not be reading the whole email but having a secondary *C.T.A.* can help you drive action from people who may not be ready for your main offer in the body of the email. This is a judgment call you'll have to make as the *Chief Marketer* based on your audience and what you're asking them to do.

> The *content* used in the various parts of the email, will affect your deliverability.

"**Deliverability**:" a factor you should be very familiar with as a marketer. You can't just assume that all emails you'll send will get delivered to the right places. You're already aware of things like *SPAM* and promotion folders filtering out marketing *content* but when discussing deliverability you're actually talking about measuring the rate at which emails you send land in your recipients real "**inboxes.**" As a legitimate business the impostor boxes are not for you, they are there to stop unsolicited people from sending bad stuff to your contacts but remember, Google and the other email providers don't always know the difference and are always looking over what you send for any clues that might indicate you are one type or the other.

So don't look or sound like *SPAM* and stay out of the *SPAM* folders. You can rely on the High Touch Conversational Marketing Method to stay below the radar and look like a person instead of a corporation or a *SPAMmer*, but if you want to be absolutely sure, here's a magic trick to be positive your email never gets "undelivered" again...

"**Opting In:**" Beyond just giving you permission to email them, most professional email service providers will allow you a way to let your contacts "opt-in" or even "**double opt-in**" to your list, meaning that by formally confirming your connection they're giving you a golden ticket straight into their *inbox* and none of your emails to them will ever get sent to the *promo or SPAM* folder from then on. This is obviously very useful for our purposes. Once requested, all they'll need to do is click a link that will come from your email service provider.

Make sure your contacts get your emails every time. Figure out if the tools you are using have this function. If they do, consider beginning the opting-in process for the people already on your list as soon as possible and

implementing a process for new leads that you meet.

"T.O.M. (Top of Mind)"

You will want to be sending out something conversational to your list of prospects and customers weekly or bi-weekly depending on the industry. By staying Top Of Mind (T.O.M.) in their inbox with regular friendly valuable *content* we will keep your authority and value fresh in their minds. Remember - a qualified lead should be in some type of pain related to the problem you solve, so get out there and address it. This is not the same thing as a newsletter...

NEWSLETTERS VS LOVE LETTERS:

Newsletters are great for community bulletins at condo complexes, shared office spaces or keeping in touch with family you don't see often, but not really suited for your marketing.

Personally I hate newsletters. Yes, hate - I know it sounds harsh. You may be different but I don't actually read them nor do the vast majority of people in the audiences I've asked so far. I wont even open them if I see the word in the *subject line* or *preview window*; even when I really like the company sending it.

"**Newsletters**" are typically tiles of content on different topics smashed into one broadcast. Even when there's something valuable in them, recipients have to look through four or five pieces of *content* they may have no interest in to find it. Who has time for that? Of course if you believe you've cracked the newsletter code, I'd love to see it - please send an example to the office.

Of all the different email types, a newsletter is a let-down from several perspectives. They're an imposition. A newsletter assumes that your contact wants to be updated on your business independent of you solving their problem and there's usually no reason to believe that; it just isn't valuable to most consumers. A newsletter is an uninspired attempt at nurture, a placebo for value, but worst of all it's inconvenient for the reader.

That being said, just like with all marketing tools,

something is often better than nothing and you can get at least some results by doing anything at all, but things will improve faster with the right strategy and mindset on your side. So if you are one of the businesses sending newsletters, next time you or someone on your team feels like blasting everybody you know, accept this challenge to send a **"love letter"** instead. A love letter is like a newsletter but better because it's more targeted.

Take those four or five topics that were going to be in the newsletter, then look at your list and roughly break it down into groups based on who is right for each topic and send out brief, conversational emails to each smaller group with the targeted *content* instead of everybody on your database getting hosed at once. They will be happy to get what you're sending because it's actually for them. That's what you do when you love someone, you don't slam them with things they aren't interested in.

Love Letter Bonus: Do some of your segmented groups fit several of the categories? Send the best one first, wait a couple days and send the next - that's the great thing about targeting: when done right, it's never *SPAM* because it's valuable to that individual based on their actual data.

> **FAQ**: *How often is too often to email my list?*
>
> As long as your recipient finds it valuable it is never *SPAM* so the better question is how often can you be valuable?

Choosing the Right Software:

Once you have a list, offers to sell, and you are out generating leads, it's time to bring in some support. Better than hiring more staff, you need a *customer relationship management* software with automation. But which one should you trust? You'll need your system to handle a few things:

- **Customer relationship management**: customers, leads, affiliates, prospects, segmentation, and notes.
- **Broadcasting:** Send one email to everyone or a particular message to a smaller group sorted by particular traits.
- **Software Automation:** Operates on "If *this* happens, then that happens" logic. We should be able to take our automation map and put it on rails making the functions happen largely automatically with minimal input from you. *"Sales on rails never fails."*
- **Opt-In Function**: Your system should ideally be able to confirm contacts email addresses to avoid the *SPAM* box.

It really does seem like there is a new email marketing provider every week so my goal isn't to help you pick the right one here necessarily, but just let you know what to look for among the more reliable options...

- Infusionsoft (Keap)
- Clickfunnels
- Hubspot
- Aweber
- Constant Contact
- Mail Chimp

These are some of the leaders when it comes to accessibility, deliverability, and reliability, but there are so many more software providers to choose from. After building funnels in every one of these systems and at least a handful more. I'll tell you that the thing you should be aware of in regards to software providers that there are a few that are worthy of your trust and a whole lot of others with hype.

Be aware that some industry specific *C.R.M.s* are notoriously difficult to use, have limited support, and can sometimes go down, taking your data with them. I strongly advise trusting an established company that won't be going anywhere and who you can rely on to help you when you need it with their software, because you will have issues - count on it.

Personally, in a head to head marketing competition I would take Infusionsoft with me any day but the truth is that I've been jaded over time after using it for so many years as a Certified Partner and later as an influencer in essentially every industry from child care, to amusement parks, to unmentionables. For me, their custom-toolbox build style lets me put together really intuitive sales machines for my clients that they can understand, but I'll also be the first to tell you they're not perfect. Especially if you are new to setting it up yourself for the first time, the learning curve is monumental for some.

You may need something with more of a "business in a box" mentality that's easy to get up and running if you are working alone and that's OK. Don't let anyone without business or automation experience talk you into the wrong system because it's cheaper or fancier or on special or anything else.

Other people's opinion means very little when it comes to marketing your business, not just because you aren't like anyone else, but because you are the one that has to operate it at the end of the day, so choose wisely.

If in doubt, ask a real automation expert you can trust to help you sort out the options and find the right fit.

CHAPTER 15

SALES 401:
Phone Marketing

"Show me the money!" (Jerry Maguire, 1996)

If email is the noble steed of your marketing, your telephone is the long sword. Trusty and good for every sticky situation, a hero would never leave home without it.

Whether you're already making thousands every month over the phone or if the thought of sales calls terrifies you, this chapter should help you get more money out of your dialing.

There really shouldn't be any *Chief Marketers* without an outgoing phone engagement strategy as the backbone of their *active sales* efforts. If your business doesn't have one yet, you should strongly consider adopting one now – right now. You have to be making nurture and sales calls to really cash in on the contacts you're working so hard for. The million (or multi-million) dollar question is "how?"

Some people claim to be the type who'll do anything to grow their business but are simultaneously scared of picking up the telephone to reach the people that need them. That's crazy. You can't be both. If you're going to be a successful marketer, you have to become *"the one who knocks."*

The clearest path to making more money today, tomorrow and until we adopt technology that just shoots messages directly into the audience's brain will likely be the telephone on the desk or the smartphone in your pocket.

> **Fact:** *your customers and leads don't have SPAM, junk, or promotion folders on their phones.*

Start with qualified phone numbers. By now you should be generating leads and have at least some of these on your list (if not, refer back to earlier chapters on identifying your traffic and collecting qualified leads). Remember, it's your responsibility of the *Chief Marketer* to collect as much information on their prospects and customers as possible and that includes basics like phone numbers. Your business relies on this data.

It's been argued that customers of physical products won't tolerate calls of any kind but I very much disagree. Whether the interaction occurred through e-commerce or at a brick & mortar store, with the right positioning you always have a good reason for a phone call to follow up.

Never forget, it's not SPAM when it's valuable. Consider implementing regular phone satisfaction surveys that end with a friendly offer or incentive for their next purchase since they are now a "**V.I.P.**"; a certain percentage of them will say yes. That's calculable growth with one step.

At the end of the day, successful results won't come from the "hey, just go do sales calls" mentality; that will turn your audience against you quicker than you think. It's truly about connecting with people who depend on you and finding ways you can make their lives better in the future. We just so happen to be using the most direct tool at our disposal: our phones.

THE "T" Word

No, using the phone in your sales process does not make you a telemarketer. Some professionals excel in person or through emails or on social media but then have the toughest time when it comes to picking up the phone and making an offer. Usually either because doing so gives them *sales call anxiety* or they think that making sales calls will somehow transform them into a **"telemarketer."** So to clear up any lingering doubt, here are some telltale signs you might be a telemarketer:

- *Cubical or "pit" environment*: If you clock in amongst 300 or more of not your freshest smelling friends to wear a headset that you have to disinfect... you might be a telemarketer.
- *"Deaf" leadership:* If you have solutions to problems but nobody cares what you think... you might be a telemarketer.
- *Strict Script:* If you are expected to read the words that are written. The words that are written on the page... you might be a telemarketer.
- *Limited Flexibility:* When you'll catch so much hell for being back 1 minute late from lunch you'll run red

lights and clip a pedestrian if your meal takes too long at Chipotle... you might be a telemarketer.

- *Emergency protocol:* Someone very close to me worked in telemarketing for a time and would share the most outrageous experiences, once claiming that the only way to make the automatic calls stop on her headset was one of two buttons on the terminal literally labeled: "Panic" or "Prayer."

Does this sound like you? Great, didn't think so.

People don't particularly like telemarketers for obvious reasons so nobody blames a marketer when they're reluctant to be lumped in as one. But since you don't fit any of the criteria above, there really isn't anything to be ashamed of in picking up the phone and making your daily call quota. A **"call quota"** is a predetermined number of phone *touches* or **"knocks"** a marketer is responsible for making on any given day along with everything else they need to be doing. Having one insures that there are always enough seeds being planted for your business to grow.

Somebody at your company needs to be working the phones and if you are the sole salesperson that somebody is you. Congratulations, you get the privilege of being the voice of your company. But one of the biggest challenge may actually be you...

"SALES CALL ANXIETY:"

Do you get anxious before you need to make a sales call? It happens to lots of people but it doesn't have to write you out of this scene, although you will need to work through it. Like a good actor or performer, protocol and familiarity are the best tools for overcoming performance anxiety.

Sometimes the more skill or knowledge you have, the more pressure there is to deliver on command. Prepare and practice, but not with a fake person, practice by making as many real sales calls as you can - consequences be damned. The *Chief Marketer* has to be the type of professional who is willing to be uncomfortable pushing themselves to new heights. You have to embrace every single sales fail as a little more experience in the "level up" bank, so just take that pressure to be perfect off of yourself right now - you are going to mess some of them up bad and it doesn't matter, there will be plenty more. It's going to make you stronger.

Putting yourself in sales spaces where you are earning real life competitive experience is the best thing you can do to sharpen your instincts. I'd had literally thousands of sales conversations before the age of 16 selling newspapers subscriptions in the hot Texas sun and thousands more by the time I'd become a sales lead renting cars at one of the busiest airports in the country. It didn't happen overnight but seeing just about every response, rebuttal, and objection you can imagine became a foundation for the skills that I have today - a pitch at a time.

I've probably made every sales mistake, twice. Quality advice can be priceless, but there is no way to achieve proficiency without experience. That's how this works: you just have to get these rookie conversations behind you and the phone is the best medium to make that happen quickly.

Environment can play a huge role in the energy of your calls and the office isn't always the best place for making sales, especially if anxiety is a factor. Here's how to create a safe sales space that works for those who are new or uncomfortable with phone sales.:

Your "Call Command Center:"

1. **Be Prepped**: Have all relevant info, contact data, details, resources, links and applicable sales materials available in front of you, ideally in one window.

2. **Isolate Yourself**: Find somewhere nobody can hear you, not even team members, family, kids, or the office janitor. Anxiety can come from fear of being overheard saying the wrong thing - consider sitting in the car with a laptop or somewhere else you know you can focus.

3. **Name Up**: Make sure you can see the name of the person you are talking to at all times. This will make you feel more comfortable using it in the conversation and help you come across as more charismatic.

4. **Notes Out**: Don't find yourself frantically searching for the right place to write "it" down. Have the right note field open and ready for your conversation. Document as much as you can while you talk. Type everything relevant said in your notes so you can refer back as needed.

5. **Plan in Hand:** Every movie, every show, every character that's ever moved you has all been working from a script or a guide. If you are going to perform like them you shouldn't be any different. Don't rely on chance, have a flow or *script* to follow.

6. **Powered:** Don't have to scramble for chargers. *Your Call Command Center* needs electricity and a stable web connection for that matter. Don't shoot yourself in the foot by having the perfect pitch they didn't hear.

If you are new to **"active sales,"** getting started is easy. Begin with the product you are focused on offering and a list of prospects to call, then work through a certain number of them every session and record both the results along with when you are going to follow up again.

Reminder: if your contact wants to buy something other than your focus then that's great but we always begin with an ideal offer for that person. Don't just call without a reason and next step for that contact firmly in mind.

Now, did you agree to follow up with them? Write down the details and set a date wherever you keep records for your next follow up. Did you send a proposal or more information over? Same thing.

Everybody needs to be touched and documented and scheduled for their next attempt: this process is known as **"working your leads."**

"SMS TEXT MESSAGES:"

You really need to fully comprehend the influence SMS text messaging has over your audience. Many people will let a call go to voicemail if they don't recognize the number and so a text message is the key to getting a message through.

> **Example:** "Hey **CONTACT NAME**! That was **ME** calling just now from **NAME OF BUSINESS.** Are you around? :)"

People aren't expecting a conversational text message from a marketer, largely because as a general rule: businesses email, friends text.

How do you really know texts are powerful? How many unanswered emails do you have right now? 100? 1000? 10,000? As of writing this I am currently the proud owner of 37,498 unopened emails and this is more common than you'd think. How many unopened text messages do you have on your phone? Chances are it's less than three.

Emails are effective when they are opened and that's why they are still a great and viable marketing platform but text messages have a better open ratio with no end in sight. After you meet a new prospect or make a new connection, don't underestimate the power of a follow up text message. At the beginning you can send these one on one to get the ball rolling but eventually you will want to explore the option of automating some of your texting because of it's successful ratio but high labor commitment.

Try mixing in an *SMS text message* as part of your sales protocol to boost engagement:

Step 1: Purchase made online → *Wait 5 minutes*

Step 2: Make "thank you"/upsell call → *Wait 5 minutes*

Step 3: Send text message thank you/follow up →

Step 4: Record activity

Step 5: Schedule next touch: Even if someone doesn't answer the phone, still set a date for when you are going to try again in your notes and on your sales calendar.

Sales 401: Phone Marketing

Phone Sales FAQs:

Should I be leaving "voicemails" on my calls?

Voicemails can go either way and results are largely based on your performance in the moment. If you choose to leave a voicemail there are a few best practices that work for my clients. Don't overshare! If you give them everything they need to know and you don't sell the idea of it in the voicemail you can be doing more harm than good. Try cultivating some mystery in your voicemail to encourage recipients to respond out of curiosity:

"Hey Brian, It's Ashley from the Book on Sales & Marketing! Just had a quick question for you so I thought I'd call since I wanted to see how you were doing anyway. Call back when you get this, talk soon."

What's the difference between Robo-calls & Auto-Dialers?

Robo-calls: These can be functional as reminders or updates for people who have registered for a webinar or any other kind of event where it's important they are prompt and if that event is marketing then technically the robo-call would be part of the sales process; but beyond these functions, robo-calling is not something many(or any) marketers should do. More than likely you will turn your contacts off in a big way and do way more damage than good.

Auto-dialers: Software or hardware that automatically calls a list, usually handing the call off to the salesperson once someone answers. If the auto-dialer plays recorded messages, it's a robo-call.

Should I call from my personal number?

Not if you can help it. Get an "office number" with one of the many tools available, but don't worry lots are inexpensive and easy to use and some even have an app for your smartphone. Google has a professional phone service that is popular among many small businesses but it's far from the only option. The most important thing is being able to see calls, messages, and the details on each contact all in one place. If you are a *solopreneur* this can be a huge help creating some breathing room between your personal and professional life so either look around yourself online or in the app store for which platform has the right features for you.

Now, with all the great phone work in motion, what happens when you get someone on the line?

You won't be learning the complete art of sales mastery and closing deals here - it's just too vast of a subject for this book of fundamentals, but you will learn the basics and that's more than enough to be effective immediately.

10 Steps for an Effective Sales Call:

1. Connect quickly when someone answers using a warm and enthusiastic tone. (Imitate talking to an old friend rather than a customer.)

2. Quickly remind the contact who you are, where you are calling from, and ask if they remember you or your company.

3. Provide them a good reason you called and ask if they would mind answering a few relevant questions.

4. Gather intelligence by leading the target with questions from your script using a compassionate energy.

5. Locate the pain relating to the problem and lead them to dive into it as thoroughly as possible.

6. Relate to their pain with a personal or anecdotal experience.

7. Walk them through a colorful scenario where their problems are solved and they are happy because of your product.

8. Ask the prospect to take action now on the phone.

9. If they respond with an **"objection,"** address the issue by providing more insight and social proof around the areas they aren't finding the right connection to your value.

10. **Repeat step 7.**

There's nothing wrong with needing to persuade your lead to act if you're making their lives better or easier with what you have for them. People are skeptical by nature and you really can't blame them for being hesitant about anything they're offered on the phone. It's your responsibility to bring clarity and certainty to their decision so they can receive the benefit.

When you can make someone excited about what their life will be like once they've taken your offer, the deals often close themselves. This is the sacred act of serving the people who need you. You don't have to trick anyone.

Not everything you plant will bloom, but with diligence people will begin to respond, slowly at first and then faster and faster - it's just a matter of how wide you are willing to cast and how long you are willing to tend.

Assume the sale: So you've done everything right and the prospect is on board with your offer, you've given them the price and you didn't get an objection. Now it's simply the little matter of the payment. Don't put extra pressure on the situation by cornering someone into saying the word "yes." Sometimes that as a gesture can be a little scary depending on the size of the commitment and the personality of the customer. Instead consider skipping right to the payment credentials to remove friction:

"That's excellent! I'm super excited for you and I know this is the best decision you could make right now, we can't wait to get started. *Did you want to put the deposit on a credit card or do you use PayPal?*"

You absolutely won't want to deploy this measure too early but you also can't be afraid to ask for the sale. After the prospect is talking about their problem and you've spent time with how much better life will be with your solution, make your move…

"Sales Sessions:" Carving out routine slots of time once, twice, three times a week or more for making sales calls and sales texts. By consistently jumping on the phone with a *quota*, a set plan, and a list of leads, you are going to be driving action but you'll also be gaining more sales experience, getting sharper and sharper as you go. You'll see what works for you and what doesn't, and hopefully

Sales 401: Phone Marketing

you'll use this knowledge to improve your sales script. Leveling up your phone sales skills will in turn improve the overall conversion rate of all your leads, making every single prospect even more valuable in your hands. *That's true mastery!*

The importance of maintaining a set sales *call quota* in your company as the *Chief Marketer* cannot be overstated. Set your allotted sales times, pull out that list of leads or *sales pipeline* and then just keep dialing until you've nailed your quota.

Within the thousands of sales coaches with thousands of different tactics on how to best close sales deals, I'm convinced that many of them can really help, especially if you're a beginner. But make no mistake, once you've nailed the basics, nothing is as useful as you gaining cold, hard, experience by offering your specific products to your audience and mapping their feedback.

Challenge yourself to make 25 offers, every day - follow the rules and I'll bet that once you see what it does for your bottom line you'll be wanting to make 50 or more. But you have to pay the blood price for the things that will serve you best. Consider every uncomfortable phone call a sacrifice on your journey to closing the biggest deal of your life.

Become "the one who knocks..."

CHAPTER 16

FUNNELS 301:
Software Automation

"It's alive! It's alive!" (Frankenstein, 1931)

What made McDonald's a giant? *Efficiency.*

"**Efficiency**" is the science of reducing waste and improving quality, and it comes from the rigorous implementation of systems and processes in your sales. The right thing in the right way with repetition, the stricter the better. It's been said that the single most impactful thing that McDonald's ever did was put a timer on the deep-fryer cooking the French fries. By taking the things that you do every day and adding a set system to them you will save your time, energy, and resources for the things that are going to be of better benefit to your business as the *Chief Marketer.*

You are already trained in the *escalation of commitment* and the different parts of the sales process, so hopefully it's clear in your mind how to map these different pieces together into a blueprint that makes sure everything and everyone has a place. When this blueprint is maintained, nobody will get lost and your sales process will be successful. But what if you want to go on vacation? What happens when you get sick?

All these welcome emails and reminders and follow ups and love letters and all of the other **"digital manual labor"** you've planned can be done automatically using business automation software. You don't need to be chained to your sales blueprint in order to be successful in sales anymore, nor do you need to hire expensive staff.

The Logic of Automation:
"When *THIS* happens, do *THAT*"

Imagine loading names and notes into a machine that then tracks and nurtures each lead through the sales journey filled with your own *content*, only letting you know when it's time for you to take action. It's possible and as someone who has been building them for years, I assure you when done properly they really work.

It's you but better, simply because it's the emails you write by hand except the sales robot sends it out on your behalf from your address. And after the appropriate time has passed it will take the next step for you too, until that lead clicks or schedules or buys, whatever you choose - all programmed in advance.

As you begin to add software automation to the different aspects of what you do in the sales blueprint, you'll find that it adds accountability and reliability far beyond just saving you resources. It's a more complete and consistent service for your customers - software automation is systems and processes on steroids.

24 hours a day, 7 days a week. No vacations, no holidays,

no sick days. Your automated software is the perfect employee, but just like any piece of technology you have to be painfully specific about what you want it to do upfront for it to work correctly.

Software automation has definitely become an important and universal part of business marketing in today's world, but that doesn't mean that most companies are doing it right. Many entrepreneurs and marketers struggle with software automation because so many sources and coaches are fixated on the advanced details of funnel building and forget to give people the base of knowledge they need to confidently get up and running. It's almost irresponsible. In truth, before you get to the software automation step, it's important to really understand your specific systems and the role they play in growing your business, so I hope you have spent time inside of mapping how your sales process works, and you've tested it manually or with someone who knows what they're doing…

There are plenty of horror stories out there of businesses building expensive automation systems that never get off the ground. This tends to begin with bad planning and only becomes worse with poor communication. Don't let this happen to you.

Here are the basic foundations of successful business automation:

"Database Management:"

Different *C.R.M.* softwares segment using different philosophies; for example, providers like Keap and Aweber use *tags* to track customers behavior. They can be set up so that when a customer makes a certain purchase, or reads a certain email, watches a video, or attends a webinar, or any range of actions, tags are added to their profile so that the data can be used to continue marketing to them more efficiently. Once tags are added, lists can be generated by the system based on behavior, target broadcasts can be used for specific groups, and eventually automatic responses can be triggered so that your sales process can become more efficient.

Other *C.R.M.* software programs use running lists to keep track of contacts and their interactions with your business. For instance, in systems like Mailchimp and Constant Contact a person can be on multiple lists at once depending on what offer they've opted into, or where the lead originated. But be conscious of who is on which list, or you may double-email contacts and that's a sure way to get them to *unsubscribe*.

I largely prefer systems that use tags because I've seen my clients have more success understanding their data in a tag format but that's a personal preference and everyone is different. More important than right or wrong, you'll need something that you will actually use.

It's critical you're able to export all of your contacts with their complete data profile at any time as a *C.S.V. file*. This is non-negotiable and choosing an automation provider that doesn't give you easy, instant access to a download of your data is essentially giving them the power to hold you hostage - so choose wisely.

Human Management & Notifications:

Your system must be able to notify the correct team member when a certain action is warranted using a form of a *task*. A **"task"** is a sales assignment designated by the system. Each campaign will benefit from having a protocol in place to notify a salesperson when a lead is active.

"Merged Fields:" Merging is the magic behind adding someone's personal information automatically into your correspondences without having to write it in yourself. These codes can be pasted into emails and texts and tell the automation software to replace it with stored personal information from your database. With the right planning, your emails can be populated automatically with things like *CONTACT FIRST NAME, COMPANY NAME, NAME OF EVENT*(met), or thousands of other specific details without you having to touch them.

Nobody on your list should be getting blast emails calling anyone *"friend,"* or *"valued customer,"* or worst of all, *"you."*

Custom fields are easy to use once you understand how they work, so be sure to spend a little time familiarizing yourself with the field functions in your marketing software tool if you are building it yourself.

Customizing your messages with personalized information will go a long way to sounding like yourself and not a robot in your automation. Most reputable providers will have this function as a standard but never guess, specifically ask for this ability before purchasing any automation software.

"Campaign Management:"

You must be able to create a sequence of coherent communication to be performed in succession over time, building the illusion that messages are being sent manually.

Campaigns begin with a goal being met and end with an action being taken.

Simple Case Study Example:

Begins with: Lead met at networking event

Ends with: Initial consultation scheduled

Max Length: 6 Weeks

1. Send Welcome email

Synopsis: Hey CONTACT FIRST NAME! Nice to meet you. It's ME from NAME OF EVENT. I'm really glad we got a chance to get connected. When is a good time to chat? Here's a *link to my calendar.* :)

Wait 2 days →

2. Reminder welcome email

Synopsis: Hey CONTACT FIRST NAME! How's it going? Just checking in, want to make sure we don't lose touch. What's your availability like this week? Here's my calendar. *Link to Calendar.*

Wait 2 days →

3. Check-in email

Synopsis: Hey again, CONTACT FIRST NAME. So busy over here since NAME OF EVENT, we haven't had a chance to get together - I'm so sorry. Thought I'd try to reach out again... Do you have some time in the next few days? I still do. Check out my calendar to see if any of my spots work for you: *link to calendar.*

Wait 5 minutes →

4. SMS Text Message reminding of emails

Synopsis: CONTACT FIRST NAME, how are you!? It's ME from NAME OF EVENT! I wanted to make sure you saw the email I just sent you.

Wait 2 days →

5. Content Email with link to Article #1

Synopsis: Hey there, CONTACT FIRST NAME! I realized that you probably haven't seen my article on *XYZ* and if you have a minute I really think you should check it out. Would love your thoughts. Read here...

Wait 2 days→

6. Email w/ testimonials about Article #1 reminder

Synopsis: I get it, you are super busy, CONTACT FIRST NAME, but I just wanted to share a few of the responses from that article I sent over a couple days ago. Wow!

(Testimonial 1:) "This article changed my life!"

(Testimonial 2:) "Who knew I was doing this wrong the whole time?"

(Testimonial 3:) "Grateful isn't the word."

I really can't believe I get to do this every day for a living. Anyway, if you missed it I'll put it here again. Or we could hop on the phone if you have the time? *Link to Calendar*

Wait until next Friday→

7. Friday Check-in email with a video link

Synopsis: Happy Friday, CONTACT FIRST NAME! Check out this video I shot not too long ago. I made it with someone like you in mind. ;)

Wait 4 days →

8. SMS Text "hi"

Synopsis: Hi, *CONTACT FIRST NAME*! Just wondering how you were. Do you have some time to talk about *XYZ*?

Wait until the next Monday morning →

9. "Is this the right email address?" email

Synopsis: Hey again, CONTACT FIRST NAME. We met a couple weeks ago at NAME OF THE EVENT and I was just reaching out again and hoping to get ahold of you. I've tried a few times and realized I may actually have the wrong email address. Will you let me know if you are getting this?

Wait 15 minutes →

10. SMS Text: Are you getting my emails?

Synopsis: Hey CONTACT FIRST NAME, I just emailed you again and got to thinking I might have the wrong email address, can you do me a favor and take a look to see if you got something from MY@EMAIL.COM? Thanks! Talk to you soon. CALENDAR LINK

Wait 3 days →

11. Set Task for Team Member to call contact

Synopsis: System alerts the appropriate team member to call the contact directly and establish connection and see why they haven't responded.

Wait X amount of time → etc...

You can continue to build onto these sequences until you have months of follow up for each lead type, source and step in the sales cycle. Best of all, as soon as someone books their conversation with you, this sequence will stop and after your conversation you can begin another sequence that picks up the conversation from there as well.

Once you've programmed these campaigns in advance, you are 100% free to generate as many leads as humanly possible knowing that you'll have sales consultations being booked on a consistent basis whether you meet 100 or 1000 or more. You could even network like crazy and then go sit on a beach to watch the sales conversations roll in as they respond to your follow up – that's the power of well-built software automation. It works for any type of lead at any step of the sales process, online or off. All of it can be preprogrammed with the right blueprint.

Integrations:

No man is an island and business software is the same way. Integrations are critical if you want your automation system to perform different types of tasks like SMS texting, scheduling, social media **<u>retargeting,</u>** and more. You will likely need a digital calendar, a sales pipeline manager, and possibly half a dozen other things as you grow depending on your industry, but don't get overwhelmed at the thought of it now. Each one happens in their own time and you don't have to rush out and buy thousands of dollars of monthly software subscriptions to begin getting results, but whatever tools you decide to implement, it's important that they play nicely with your primary automation software.

It doesn't actually matter as much which particular software you choose for your funnel automation, as much as it does that you are following the rules and you've planned accordingly.

If building your own software automation, be aware that your first campaign is probably going to be bad. Your first five may be bad. If you don't have a technical or programming background, this will be a frustrating process even if you're lucky, but just know that upfront. However, that doesn't mean you won't succeed, so if you've chosen this path you just can't give up before you figure it out.

This book is about sales and marketing fundamentals and truthfully there are thousands of more intricacies involved in every chapter and more. Per the 80/20 rule, my focus is to give you the top 20% of what you need to get 80% of the results. But that doesn't mean everything can or should be done yourself. It's just too much to expect from one person.

I don't believe that all business owners or marketers should do their own software automation, I just don't. As the late Mitch Hedberg once joked, "It's like if you worked

Funnels 301: Software Automation

your ass of to become the best chef and they turn around and say 'Great! Can you farm?'"

Learning to market your business is hard enough without adding the extra pressure of platform knowledge or bugs or programming. The learning curve is just too vast. It's a technical process that can absolutely be learned with diligence but if you are carrying out the steps you're developing here, your time as the *Chief Marketer* is much better spent elsewhere.

Yes, 20% of marketers will be able to navigate it with help and the top 20% of those will see success alone, but the larger majority will just find themselves frustrated with sunk time building something they'll never really use and either pay to have it redone by an expert or worst of all, skip it, ruining their companies potential sales capacity before it ever got the chance to succeed.

If you need support, have questions, or if you need to know more about the right tools for your business, visit:

www.TheBookOnSalesAndMarketing.com/Tools

CHAPTER 17

CONTENT 301:
Your Brand & Your Bible

"The secret's in the sauce"
(Fried Green Tomatoes, 1991)

There are some branding experts I would absolutely trust with my businesses. These gurus are intuitive, gifted, professional, and deliver results, but they're also expensive - very expensive. But even if you can't afford a guru, you shouldn't be afraid of getting started on your own.

If you are planning on overseeing your own branding then here's great news: your **<u>brand</u>** is not a living breathing thing you have to tend, it's a set of rules you follow every time you produce content. The better your rules, the better your brand. Of all the ways to spend a marketing budget, branding is not necessarily on the top of my list as an in-tune marketer or business owner should be able to develop most of it themselves with a robust target map and their top 20% in mind.

Nobody should know your business better than the *Chief Marketer*, so it's best they're involved whenever possible. If you've found yourself at a place in your business where you have basics like a profitable list, automation, and a WordPress website covered and you can afford a real brand expert, they can absolutely bring the larger element of magic that an average person just usually doesn't have the eye for. But for the most part, by focusing on the problem you solve and building structure, authority and testimonials, your colors and font won't be so important to future customers. Consistency and value is what really matters. But how do you maintain brand consistency across multiple platforms?

You'll need to develop a strong **"brand bible."** A brand bible is the reference point or guide for everything you make in the business. It will be the core resource used by you or anyone you hire to easily create designs for ads, emails, landing pages, flyers and anything else your sales process requires. Your brand bible will have the individual elements you'll need housed and documented in detail all in one place. By creating this one centralized resource, everyone will be on the same page, allowing you to build a strong, consistent look and *smell* for your brand over everything you do.

It should include your primary colors, passive colors, active colors, *action color,* and other signature color information. It will include the fonts that your business uses in its written materials, in its menus, on its website, and everywhere else; this will typically include a headline font, subtitle font, a standard text font, and an action font.

CONTENT 301: Your Brand & Your Bible

You'll need a library of current acceptable photos, backgrounds, and logo source files to be used in relation to your branded materials.

Include a vocabulary of power words and phrases associated with your brand: *stunning, reliable, affordable, luxurious, exclusive, relaxed, etc.* This collection of unique power words will help copy writers or team members create consistent and powerful messages quickly that actually sound like your business.

All of this and everything else that is vital to the personality of your brand goes in the brand bible.

> **Note**: *Colors are often recorded in* **"hex code"** *format to make sure you are getting the exact shade of the color you're looking for. You will see them presented as #f4d942 or #941be5. There are free sites online that will let you upload a photo and then select the hex code of the color you need.*

The brand bible is infallible because good or bad, it's how the company has collectively decided to represent itself. Until the powers that be adjust your brand bible, everything needs to be within its guidelines. That means once you've set these rules in place it's critical that everyone on your team follow it religiously, including yourself. Yes, your brand bible will change over time, but hopefully more like the U.S. Constitution and less like the *Batman movie* reboots - growing and evolving, not torn down and redone every few years.

When you see solid bright red behind a white handwritten scrolling font, your brain screams Coca Cola. If you're from Texas and you see orange and white stripes together your mouth waters for a Whataburger. That's because their brand has been consistently tied to those elements for years and they've accomplished it by leading with value and sticking to the script.

Over time you are going to need different websites, different marketing messages, different landing pages, physical prints, signs, displays, and so many other pieces to this marketing puzzle, but no matter how many you add they all need to "smell" the same.

"Ad scent:" Smell is often the sense attributed to how a piece of marketing feels in relation to the rest of the brand. If a visitor were to be clicking around your financial planning website where everything is designed in neutral colors but then find themselves on the *"about us"* page that's bright bubblegum pink, it's likely to stop them in their tracks. Even if it's not a deal-breaker, they will take notice of the inconsistency. We would say that something "doesn't smell right." Sometimes these things are obvious like color but other times they happen subliminally due to smaller details like an alien font, an out of place vocabulary term or anything that looks like it doesn't belong with the rest of your brand.

"Logo:" Logos are the signature art you use to represent your business but just because they're important doesn't mean they have to be expensive. If you do not have a graphic designer on your team and you don't know where to start with getting a new logo or updating the one you have, www.Fiverr.com can be a solid place to start looking around for the style you want but be warned: there are so many options and different people presenting themselves as experts on Fiverr that are really just providers of templates that you might want to choose a trusted designer instead so you don't run the risk of seeing your logo somewhere else with another name slapped over it.

Graphic Design: The best thing you can do for stronger graphic design in your branding is build as detailed a brand bible as possible and then try to develop a relationship with a graphic designer or expert who shares your vision, even if they're a contractor. Nothing is more frustrating than hunting for the right talent on Fiverr.com or anywhere else for that matter when you need to have a sales flyer or promotion page done.

Video: Helping people achieve better video and visuals was my full time occupation for many years and I've literally made hundreds of videos for clients in my career. I've seen what works and what's forgettable. Although this topic could be a book in itself, let's look at the basics of how to make better sales video to support our sales efforts.

All sales & marketing videos should include:
1. **Who you are.**
2. **What you do.**
3. **Why the viewer should care.**
4. **What you want them to do now.**

Video is one of the most versatile mediums your business can harness and you can't afford to wait any longer to get started using it if you aren't already.

FAQ: *What camera is best for my business?
If having the right camera is holding you back from making your first videos, skip it and start on your phone. The best camera in the world is the one you have on you and there are more than enough tools in your pocket to be dangerous. Obviously as you go on to shoot longer videos more often, you will probably want something that will keep up without the slow download times of a smartphone.
My weapon of choice is a mid-ranged Sony camcorder under $800. Camcorders are great because they don't need lenses and are designed for shooting on the fly. They are light, nimble, boot up quickly and perform well in low light. Camcorders also usually have superior battery life.*

<u>Performing on Camera:</u> Struggling with delivering your "*lines?*" There's nothing wrong with using a teleprompter – the faster you can get videos complete, the better – but teleprompters can be a pain to load and operate, especially on a tight schedule.

I've found that it can be way easier for most experts to opt for using a cue card with main points written in big font with a *fat black magic marker - a felt pen*. When it comes to video content, shorter is often better than longer. People's attention spans are short so unless it's a training or deep exploration on a particular topic, keep it under five minutes in length, but this depends on the platform and the specific purpose of the content so choose wisely.

"<u>Video Batching</u>:" Filming a bunch of videos at once. You're already on location, dressed and have the camera rolling, what else can we shoot that will be valuable?

It's more cost effective per video the more you can pack into one shooting session. Don't worry so much about perfect, people are going to be impressed at the volume of video you have available and it will help them to feel like they really have a feel for your brand.

If you are filming videos yourself, always frame the shot a little wider than you intend on using because, while you're always able to zoom in some in editing, you can't zoom out.

If you use Mac, iMovie is a perfectly acceptable editing tool; the same goes for Windows Movie Maker – whatever gets you the results is the right answer.

My editing platform of choice has been Adobe Premiere and the suite of Adobe softwares for years since film school. Adobe makes good creative products but all of them take training. If editing on an app is easier for you,, do whatever it takes to make it happen.

"**Content silo:**" Located within the *brand bible,* the Content Silo is where you keep a list of the descriptions and locations of every graphic, offer sheet, video, brand photo and logo variation with their related source files all in one place. Often segmented by type, a content silo is where the marketer goes when they need to create materials but don't want to spend a ton of time or money reinventing the wheel.

Some businesses have more assets than they are aware of and keeping track of what is already in possession is the first big step to content management.

Hungry for Video: Every time you get the attention

of more than a few people about solving the problem you solve is also a great opportunity to gather valuable video content for your marketing. Whenever you can get them, these and other videos of you in action can be edited together into bigger, more powerful pieces without hiring an expensive production crew to come and shoot you a video.

This should be a vital part of your docu-content strategy, gathering video on the fly, but you must be vigilant. If you're on a budget, do whatever it takes to capture the shot. Don't be afraid to ask a bystander to record a couple minutes for you that you can use. "*A year from now you'll be glad you started today.*"

FAQ: What's the difference between shooting video on my camera vertically versus horizontally?

If you are shooting video on your phone camera, always hold it horizontally so that the image fills the whole frame. All smart phone cameras have sensors that pick up the data passed through the lens but a lot of phones only use half of the sensors capacity when video is recorded vertically. Get more of the action and hold your camera horizontally.

Audio is king: my audio engineering professor in college often said "people see with their ears" and time after time he's been proven right. People will accept bad video and great audio in a way they won't forgive bad audio with good video. I've had very big projects ruined on multiple occasions due to bad sound. Make sure that whoever is in the video is miked with either a personal

CONTENT 301: Your Brand & Your Bible

recorder like a **"lavaliere"** or an unobstructed **"shotgun microphone."**

Your brand doesn't just end with things you can see. If you produce a podcast, use radio commercials or even background tracks or **"stingers"** in your videos, you can use the same audio cues and music to create brand identity for listeners as well.

Producing Effective Video:

1. Title: don't forget a good title on all marketing media. Depending on the platform, the viewer may be able to see the title either at the beginning or the end so don't name anything *"Sales Pitch Video 2.6."*

2. **"Script:"** (Specifically a **"video script"**) copy written to be turned into content. Audio can have scripts, videos should have scripts and *animation*s are almost impossible to produce without scripts because you will need a canvas to indicate what visuals need to accompany the message where.

3. Tone: you'll always need to be able to communicate the distinct tone of the media you're making because unless you are doing it all yourself, you never want your creative experts to have to guess. Excited? Overjoyed? Serious? Is it inviting? Challenging? Quirky? Fun? Does your video have attitude? All of these different tones are great directions that will help the creatives give you visuals that fit and the talent delivers exactly what you need to connect with and persuade the audience.

4. A **"voice-over:"** many effective videos have a

"voice-over" or someone reading your message to help guide the visuals along. Who is that going to be? It can be the business owner or anyone at the company of course, but chances are you are going to want to choose a professional so that you don't have to worry about any of the technical stuff like recording audio or balancing levels or even cutting it. Once you have a tone and a script, explain to your voice actor or producer what they are trying to convince the listener to do and let them make some magic.

5. <u>C.T.A.</u>: like every good piece of marketing content, what you want the audience to do next needs to be clear whether it be something specific like "click the button," or "subscribe," to "Buy Now."

<u>Bookends:</u>" bookends are branded video clips with your logo used at the beginning and end of larger video content to give an added boost of quality or **<u>production value</u>**." Great for **<u>talking head videos</u>**" where you or anyone is speaking straight into the camera, bookends usually incorporate your brand colors and have a smooth animated transition into the main content. Simple videos can be effective but visually flat and will sometimes get lost among all the other exciting media out there. Starting the same talking head video with a bookend to catch someone's attention and then another again at the end fading to black will make your whole message feel more professional to the viewer overall.

"**<u>Animation</u>**" is one of the most powerful and universally effective forms of video because it transcends language and culture. Everybody loves animation.

"**Whiteboard videos**" are exactly what many businesses need to affordably get started in the video space without worrying about lighting or backgrounds or audio or performing in front of a camera. Simply deliver a script to an expert along with your *Brand Bible* and tone.

The supercharge that animation gives businesses is clear and anyone who understands the influence that animation has over people would want to incorporate it on their home page as soon as possible. We've found visitors spend on average 33% longer on pages that have video than ones that don't. But beyond just a video of someone talking to the camera, an animated or *whiteboard* video can do amazing things for the visitors excitement to work with you. In the hands of the right animator, your business can become fun and engaging like never before; the trick is finding the right talent that understands your vision and won't gouge you on the production. If a picture is worth a thousand words, a good animation video is worth millions.

For examples of successful bookends, animations, whiteboard and other types of useful videos visit:

www.TheBookOnSalesAndMarketing.com/Video

CHAPTER 18

WEB FUNDAMENTALS:
Sites, Landing Pages & Google

"If you build it, they will come"
(Field of Dreams, 1989)

An impressive website is very important to your sales efforts. It's just less important than your social media presence and less important again than a strong database. It's possible to gain a lot of traction with even a simple WordPress website if you have a *delicious offer* in hand and you're reaching the right people with the right message. Even e-commerce websites that do their business primarily online can sometimes get away with basic pages simply because their audience just want somewhere easy to check out. But before long, every growing business will need a professional website that represents their company the way it deserves to be represented and it's wise to have a working knowledge of the fundamentals if you want to have a reliable plan in place when that time comes.

> **FACT:** *A ship captain doesn't have to batten down the hatches, hoist the masts or wench the anchor, but they'd better know how all of those parts work together in unison to sail the ship or they won't be a very good captain.*

Websites are intricate and complicated networks of connections on the back end and most website experts are going to have a lot to say about **"search engine optimization (S.E.O.)"** and **"meta-data"** and yes those will absolutely have a huge impact down the line, but the truth is that for many small businesses, your average website visitor will probably won't be coming to you cold from Google but from interacting somewhere else and getting **"redirected"** or flat-out finding your website on purpose. when that's the case, spending time or money on making sure all of your images and pages are optimized, have the right **"backlinks"** and so on might not make you more money in the short term – unless you're really driving heavy traffic from somewhere like paid ads or content. For most small businesses, their website is more of a digital business card than it is an actual cold-traffic magnet.

For that reason, there's no shame in choosing an easy website builder like Wix.com or Squarespace.com if it's your first site, even if they do come with their own challenges. However, despite its complexity, **"WordPress"** is the superior website builder. When clients can afford it, it's always a smarter choice over the others at any stage. But be warned that unless you are technically savvy or have some coding experience, you may struggle to build a Wordpress site yourself, even with a theme or **"skin."**

Top 6 Reasons WordPress is the superior website platform:

1. *Secure: There is always a risk of third party website platforms exposing your credentials. While you may not think the risk is that scary due to your business' size, if you value your site's security, choose Wordpress.*

2. *Handles all media types: Website builders give you drag and drop tools but those tools only have so many options and sometimes won't accept certain file types or sizes. WordPress has functions to handle all media and file types.*

3. *Integrates with everything: All marketing software tools are built with WordPress in mind so you never have to guess: Does it integrate with WordPress? Yep, it does.*

4. *100% customizable: The only limit is your imagination.*

5. *Google Loves WordPress: S.E.O. is basically a measure of how easy it is for Google to find and recommend your site and the friendlier your website is with it the better.*

6. *Low monthly cost!: Once your site is built, it only*

needs to be hosted - *no subscription payment.*

Regardless of the platform you end up choosing, there are some vital organs in every successful business website.

A Websites "Vital Organs:"

"Home Page:" The brain of your website, the home page gives visitors a general overview of who you are, the problems you solve, and more importantly, what you believe. You are more than the products or services you provide and there are unique reasons why you are the best fit for the audience you've curated so make sure it's clear right up front on the home page. The home page should give easy access to all of the content and other pages on the site, often in a sidebar or dropdown menu If you have one good video about you and what you do, this is often where it should go.

"About Us:" Important appendages, "About Us" are the arms you use to hug your visitors. People want to know who they are doing business with and this is the place where you tell the journey of how your company came to be the leaders in your space or offer the great products that you do. The *"about us"* page is about credibility and human connection, so bring them close. What is your mission? What do you and your team wake up excited to do every day? The only people visiting this page are considering taking action with you in some capacity so keep that in mind when you sit down to write this copy. Build trust. What about your company might bring them over the fence?

"Testimonials:" *Social Proof* - the lungs. People want

to see that what you do has worked for other people and is truly one of the spaces where the more you have the better. Don't be shy here, there's nothing wrong with finding every nice thing anyone has ever said about your business and putting it up on the testimonial page of your website. I would even challenge you to contact old customers and get new testimonials from their past experiences. This is your opportunity to make it clear beyond a shadow of a doubt that what you do works for your clients. Shout your lungs out.

Text testimonials are great, text testimonials with the person's picture next to it are better, and video testimonials are the crown jewels. So let me remind you again to always be collecting these at all times, they are more valuable than gold.

C.T.A.: Arteries that belong on every page. What do you want someone to do immediately upon consuming the content in front of them... *Click, schedule, buy, download?* That needs to be crystal clear everywhere they go. Buttons and links are both great options for encouraging someone to take an action. These opportunities for next steps on each page should be pumping life blood to the offer pages.

"The Action Button:" *"Sign up," "Subscribe," "Download," "Join."* A clickable button on a site or webpage, all *action buttons* have a short prompt and should stand out from whatever background they are on. You never want someone visiting your site to miss it. My rule is to make the button a color that's in line with the brand but that you won't find anywhere else on the page. This is where you refer back to your brand bible where you've stored this **"action color."** Orange is often a good action color because it's bright and fits with many pallets, but if one of your brand colors are already orange you'll need another color to make it stand out on the page.

"Pop ups:" Even if you don't know the term, you've certainly seen them at work. A pop up interrupts your viewing of a website or content to make an offer and usually provides only two options - click the offer or find the X to close it. Pop ups also sometimes employ charged questions that turns refusing your offer into a statement about themselves:

Example: Fitness Article, "5 Facts for Eliminating love handles"	
Ready to finally get rid of that stubborn muffin top?	
No, I love being fat	YES!

If you hate them, you're not alone.. The fact is that they work. A pop up makes you look at someone's offer whether you like it or not, it's the ultimate in disruption.

Example: Cooking blog, "Grandma Arlene's Famous Chicken Dumplings "	X
Get Chef Ryan's 7 Guarded family recipes for $1	
Download now	

"Bio" of the CEO/President/ or Owner: The backbone or spine of your whole website, the business owner or entrepreneur's authority in the industry can't be underestimated. Use this biography page to soothe the potential customer who needs reassurance that they are in the best hands. This is not your life story necessarily, only what you can position directly behind how you became a passionate and knowledgeable leader in your industry. At the end of the day, people want to do business with people they know, like and trust so don't forget to include a great photo of yourself as well.

Website photos: Every page must have photos but not just any photos. Your website photos are more important than most and if you don't have some you love already, consider getting professional shots done. Remember, many of your visitors either haven't met you yet or may never meet you and so these are the photos they'll use to interpret what you do, your energy, your attitude, your presence. Professional photographers use Photoshop and heavy editing to make their clients look their best so if you are one of those people who hate how they look, a professional photographer is a smart choice.

"Contact Us:" Your website's ears. It's important your contact us is welcoming and has a clear greeting that fits at least 80% of your visitors. Your contact us page hosts the "Contact Us Form" and that form isn't always built inside Wordpress or the website builder itself but is often actually a form made inside an automation software like Infusionsoft(Keap) and simply hosted on the website. By embedding the automated form into the website this way, everyone who submits will be updated directly into your *C.R.M.* and thusly a preprogrammed welcome sequence to start doing some of the education and initiation legwork for you will kick into action. That lets you add functions like allowing visitors to select a "type" that will designate them – things such as, "Potential customer", "Current customer", "partner", "affiliate", or whatever is appropriate for your business. That segmentation can determine the type of automatic response they get. Your contact us page is a critical part of your website.

Main Sales Page: The sales page is the heart of your business and all other pieces should be encouraging the visitor to get to this point and take action. Where the rubber meets the road… Do you sell tires? This is the page where people can either buy tires or schedule an appointment to come buy tires. Restaurant? This is where the "buy gift cards," "order now," and "make reservation" buttons live. Coaching? You need options like "Join Mastermind," "Download Guide" or "Buy My Book." Even if your business doesn't sell something directly from your website your sales page should focus on an offer or offers that will prompt them to take action.

When someone buys or takes action on your site, they're often *redirected* to a **"Thank You page,"** a place where they're not only thanked but typically also given some confirmation details on whatever they just agreed to. These pages are a great place to reaffirm that the lead is on the right path and should tell them what to expect from you next, whether that be an email or something else.

> **Pro-tip**: Weaponize your Thank You pages. If most landing page and website C.T.A. submissions have a Thank You page built in when submitted, let's make sure it does something aside from just saying "thank you." Give these engaged individuals another opportunity for getting more of you right then and there… more content, a link to your calendar, a special upsell offer, something. Never underestimate the power of a good call to action on a Thank You page. *"Strike while the iron is hot"*

It shouldn't surprise you to discover that many of your

website viewers and landing page visitors will be doing so from some kind of mobile device. Phones and tablets are the most common tools for browsing and we've reached a point where it's more important to have a beautiful mobile design than it is a traditional desktop. Obviously you don't want either to be bad, but build your websites with mobile as your primary focus and keep your engagement higher than those who don't. This is part of understanding your audience and their behaviors. Many audiences will be primarily using mobile to browse, what about yours?

FAQ: Is a website the same as a **"landing page?"**

No. Although they're both web pages your business uses in the sales cycle hosted on their own unique domains, they serve two different purposes. A website is home base for your business online and has everything you do on display in a (hopefully) easy to navigate format, whereas landing pages are blunt sales instruments used to offer a visitor one thing and one thing only.

You likely only need one website; you likely need multiple landing pages. A landing page doesn't have links or buttons to your website or other content. It doesn't have Facebook, LinkedIn, or any other social media buttons for that matter, only a submission button. A landing page focuses on one offer and one singular question: "Are you in?"

The only ways to get out of a landing page should be to act, hit the back button, or to close the tab. This isn't crazy, it's because this method reduces the amount of visitors who get distracted: a certain amount of the population are habitual readers and will continue to look around as long as there is more information to be consumed and considered. These people won't buy until they feel like they got the whole picture, but if you've done a good job on your content they will have a lot to look at - what follows is usually indecision. They will leave your tabs open on their browser for days or weeks until they likely forget about you entirely. Modern problems require modern solutions and this problem gave birth to the innovation of the landing page as we know it today: providing just enough information to make a decision and then forcing someone to decide whether they're going to pull the trigger.

The Google Index:

You have to make sure your website is set up to appear correctly in the **"Google Index,"** the list that populates when somebody uses their search bar. We want it to not only find you, but think you are relevant to what the searcher is looking for.

Many business owners assume this happens automatically and are then shocked weeks or months later to find out they've been unregistered the whole time. Don't let this be you.

Someone needs to actually pop the *internet hood* and install the different parts that the search engine will be trying to line up with audience's search terms. Furthermore, you have to define what is visible when you appear in the search list.

This can be tricky for people who aren't experienced in the realm of Google, so if you know your website isn't properly indexed or you don't know but definitely don't want to fix it alone, reach out and get someone to help.

www.YourBusiness.com:

If you haven't purchased your web **"domain"** yet, buy it as soon as you can. If "www.YourBusiness.com" is unavailable, consider adding your city name on either side of it.

Example:

If www.**PipeWorks**.com is taken, try

"www.**LosAngelesPipeWorks**.com" or

"www.**PipeWorksLosAngeles**.com."

But what if you don't just do business locally? Yes, you could come up with an alternative like "www.ThePipeWorks.com" or "www.RealPipeWorks.com," although there are other options. You are not restricted to just ".com" for the domain extension of your website.

You've probably seen businesses @ ".net," ".org," and maybe even things like ".io," and they are becoming more prominent as the ".com's" are snatched up. The most interesting thing about these extensions is how they aren't just cosmetic, they are official registered labels that have actual meanings and are generally associated with countries, industries, and specific behaviors invented out of necessity in the hopes of keeping some sense of organization as the internet grew - that's not how it's largely turned out. Surprise.

".bet" isn't the Black Entertainment Television domain, it's an extension for bloggers and blogging, ".tv" sounds like it's short for "television," although it's actually the domain extension for the people of Tuvalu, a country in the Pacific Ocean. But why can't I host my line of ethnic hair care products at .bet? How about putting my web series at wwwMyWebseries.tv?" You can.

Consumers don't know this domain code (.tv) belongs to a small Polynesian island and will just assume it's an official extension for professional media.

This is just one more tool that can be adopted by the resourceful marketer. There is much less competition for these odd domain extensions and you can buy them at the same place you buy the ".com" domains; they're sometimes cheaper, so explore. Here are just a few:

.agency	.boutique	.club	.lol
.accountant	.business	.cool	.men
.airforce	.cash	.dental	.ninja
.army	.cleaning	.lawyer	.online

Yes, you can buy domains with extensions @ things like ".army" and nobody will stop you. What can you do with that power? Does your business serve people in the military? Show your support and make a special landing page with a promotion just for them. So who do you serve that might be ripe for a special offer attached to a custom domain page?

You can also buy catchy domains and *redirect* the traffic back to your main website or a primary sales page. That makes it easier to get people to visit your pages and the easier it is for someone to remember your domain name the better, so get creative. But visiting is one element, and getting them to make a purchase is another. With *e-commerce* you can capture that momentum into dollars. on the spot

E-commerce" is the deployment of a digital store on your website where your traffic can shop or make actual purchases without your assistance, ideally with an automated fulfillment and follow up process to go along with it. Products, programs, services, training, all of it can be sold from your website with an e-commerce platform.

Although it's not for every business, for many, e-commerce is the backbone of their offerings; but even for them, adding additional "sourced products" can be a great supplement for the things they already sell. If you are cultivating a certain audience for what you do, consider adding additional external products that will make their lives better in a store of your own. If you are doing it well it should feel natural. It's a great way to add more value and make additional revenue at the same time. Think of it like your own mini-Amazon store filled with stuff that is just right for the audience you are already building.

In an effective e-commerce purchasing process, a customer should buy, be presented with another offer immediately, and then get follow up through your *C.R.M./ Automation* system where everyone is being tracked, organized and stored.

Having an e-commerce store without automation in fulfillment and follow up is a recipe for disaster. For most businesses at the point they are incorporating e-commerce, they will also likely need an expert automation and integration specialist to build a front end and back end process for ongoing success and sustainable customer satisfaction. This is crucial because without a system you likely won't even know you have a problem until it's too late.

The reality is simple: we live in a digital world where

your future customers make decisions to work with you or not based on what they see online. At the end of the day, your business deserves a website that shows off who you really are and that you, as a marketer can be proud to share with leads - that confidence alone will improve sales.

There's no doubt that referring new traffic to a site that impresses them will help you make more money than one that doesn't, no matter who it is you serve, so don't wait on a great website if you can help it.

Learn more about the right websites for
every business and budget:

www.TheBookOnSalesAndMarketing.com/Tools

CHAPTER 19

NETWORKING 201:
Visibility & Pay for Play

"You're gonna need a bigger boat" - (Jaws, 1975)

There are many more opportunities for you inside groups and gatherings beyond just as an attendee. With your WordPress website in place, crafted offers ready for sale, and a system to welcome, educate, and initiate new contacts, you're ready to start generating batches of leads instead of just one at a time.

"**Sponsorship:**" Most organizations, groups, and associations have opportunities to sponsor their different events and once you learn the ropes you may want to consider moving up to that level. These paid spots are great when the right business finds the right audience, but don't force it if you aren't positive these people are that audience for you.

Often you'll get a table, commonly called a *booth*,

usually an introduction and sometimes a couple minutes to talk depending on the function itself and how much you've paid. Obviously the more time you can spend in front of everyone as a sponsor the better it is for your authority and you can expect that to boost your return on investment overall. Push for as much as you can get. Some spots are more affordable than you'd think and if you find yourself at an event full of your target audience just go ask the organizer how much the sponsorship opportunities are - you may be surprised.

Don't underestimate the power of a special offer "just for this group," even if it's your standard sponsorship promotion with the name changed for their benefit.

"**Booths:**" Working your *booth* doesn't just mean decorating your table and standing next to it some. You actually have to have a plan and execute it while you're there. Your goal is to connect with everyone who can possibly use what you do and get their information to follow up. You might even make some sales right then and there, but don't forget that the primary mission is to fill your list with all potential buyers in the room and that'll take someone *working your booth*.

"**Working the booth**" is easiest when distilled to three main phases:

Disrupt: A large percentage of people are programmed by years of bad solicitation to try their best to walk by anyone at a booth without making eye contact - don't take it personally. You have to get their attention. Often you'll see giveaways, handouts or contests used as lead magnets (although these strategies are still passive by definition and really don't guarantee anyone will stop long enough to see what you have on their own). You don't always have to spend money to get someone to talk to you but I won't say it doesn't help. Everybody loves something free, but if you're deploying that strategy be sure that whatever you are giving away is valuable enough for a qualified prospect to happily swap for their contact information, otherwise your **"swag"** will either sit there on the table or vanish with nothing to show in return.

Try asking traffic a **"loaded question."** A *loaded question* presents the mystery of value while stopping a potential lead long enough to make a connection and give you a sales path regardless of their response.

Engage: Follow up whatever their response is with other fact finding questions leading toward pain they're suffering in the area of the problem you solve. Once they are on topic, keep them talking long enough to feel comfortable with you before making your move.

Example:

Loaded Question: *"Hi, there! Quick question - are you using videos in your sales process?"*

If response is yes: *"Awesome! Can you show me anything you've had made recently? How has the response been?"*

If response is no: *"Well hang on a second, why not? It's too expensive? Is it just too much of a headache for you to worry about right now?"*

Collect: You need their contact information but more importantly you should get them on the calendar with a firm appointment if they are a really good lead. Don't rely on people giving you their business card alone. If you suspect they are a highly qualified prospect and they don't have a digital calendar handy, be persistent: get them to agree to a tentative time and text them right then with the details as confirmation.

> **Sales Pro-Tip**:
>
> Don't underestimate the power of Facebook messenger or any other direct messaging tool inside your LinkedIn or other social media. Sometimes the easiest way to connect with your target is where their friends are talking to them. A casual "hello," or "nice to meet you" may get the conversation started way faster than a pitch.
>
> But whatever you do, never try to offer anyone something in the first message, that's a recipe for death that will likely get blocked or ignored. Instead, start by explaining who you are and why you're excited to connect, then let the conversation naturally move toward working together if it's a good fit.

Warning: Many sponsors lose money on their sponsorships, they seem to complain about it at nearly every event but be assured that's not everyone. It just takes a good marketer and it wasn't them that day.

There are really only two reasons a sponsorship fails: either it wasn't the right audience or whoever working it didn't do a good job connecting. You can't sit behind your *booth* and you can't be on your phone or computer. If you have the right offer and the right audience, the only thing stopping your *booth* from being successful is your willingness to get out there and disrupt the traffic walking by. So go get them, Marketer.

Speaking: The next rung of event sponsorship. You know how to generate activity inside an event and at a *booth*, but now consider getting in front of the group as the expert. Take your best piece of content and deliver it as a talk or training. People will naturally see you as an authority and want to work with you.

Make no mistake: you can be a speaker! You can even **"Speak to Sell."** You don't have to be a professional speaker or in a guild to make money sharing your expertise. You don't even have to be good, just solve a problem well. Thousands of groups filled with your perfect target are looking for speakers right now at this very moment, you simply have to make yourself visible and ask to fill those spots. Your most relevant article, guide, training, or checklist can become a 15-minute presentation that groups of your potential customers will love, value, and remember. Almost any strong piece of marketing content should be able to become a 15 minute talk if you've incorporated the *P.S.P.S. model* and that will smoothly capture leads in front of the right crowd with a landing page for them to opt-in at.

I don't teach speaking or its many intricacies, and there are some great speaking coaches out there, but I will say that it's an effective tool for building authority and bringing in some great traffic.

Don't forget to use the *P.S.P.S model* throughout your talk just like in your *content* and set them up for coming to you for the next step of their solution.

Passion and enthusiasm are your two best weapons on any stage just like in your marketing *content*, so get fired up and knock em' dead with your knowledge.

Teaming Up: Speaking and sponsoring are one

thing but attaching your company to an established organization is brand positioning on a whole other level. Once you've sponsored and been around enough to build some authority, consider connecting with the right groups to find ways you can team up.

Ask the organizers if they want to throw a special event date together with you on a certain topic or for a particular interest. How about to highlight a charity or cause? When you are the star or co-star of the show you set the rules. If they say yes, note the collaboration likely won't be free but if done well, hosting your own event can be as good as printing leads.

Note that if you are hosting or co-hosting an event you will likely be at least partially responsible for putting *butts in seats*, that's fine. You fill rooms with the same sales and marketing skills we use for our businesses:

Product (ticket) + **Lead** (Past attendee list & leads) + **Sales Process** (Emails, texts, calls, Social Media)

= **Revenue** ($$$)

To fill your event, consider bringing in other supplementary businesses or speakers related to the special topic and giving them a quota for attendees they are responsible for putting in the room in exchange for the opportunity. Just don't mistakenly bring in your competition.

With a little creativity and hard work you can throw a great community event that will launch your authority, stuff your database, and excite new prospects to work with you in a whole new way.

Networking is such a critical part of the business experience and of being an effective leader for that matter.

We are so much stronger together, but always seem to find ourselves with the customers, connections, and resources we need right next door with no access to them.

It doesn't have to be that way - your network and authority are the key to unlocking higher quality opportunities for your business.

CHAPTER 20

SOCIAL MEDIA 201:
Advertising & Local Link Networks

"I have always depended on the kindness of strangers"
(A Streetcar Named Desire, 1951)

Social media investments are sometimes tough to quantify, especially when it comes to development of *content*. Did that article you wrote or that video or motivational quote or graphic actually influence a specific purchase? Maybe not, but collectively all of these quality posts add up to authority which in itself will lead to more sales over time. Social media is a cumulative game by nature and earning eyeballs takes work. Although the most obvious way around this is to whip out your wallet and pay for exposure, that's not the only option for the resourceful marketer...

Facebook and other social media platforms target audiences using networks made of millions of micro-connections to determine who likes what and who might know who - they're always analyzing new activity for patterns within different communities. Every platform is littered with little triggers that add notes to the back end of your profile when you activate them with a click or a visit or a like. That in turn is what marketers like us depend on when asking Facebook to show a promotion to all the "cross-fit moms" of Walnut, California.

Once upon a time, everybody who liked your business page would see your posts in their Facebook feed whenever you had new activity. But as Facebook has gotten hungrier for ad dollars that model has shifted, making it harder and harder to get in front of the people who've already liked your business and harder still to get to strangers.

If you have 1000 likes, your post may only get to 200 or 250 of your fans **<u>organically,</u>** or without paying for it. If reach is the measure of people seeing any individual piece of *content* in their feed, a **<u>boost</u>** is Facebook's term for putting advertisement dollars behind that post to get more reach without starting a campaign or doing much else. It will just tell you upfront how many people they will show it to for how much money. Unapologetic pay for play.

You can exploit their system manually using a **<u>local-link network</u>** instead:

Start with 9 of the closest local business owner or marketing friends you've made networking in your area and reach an agreement to work together to leverage each other's social media audiences. Each of you may have

SOCIAL MEDIA 201: Advertising & Local Link Networks

access to however many hundreds or thousands of people who've liked your business pages alone, but together you have quite a large pool of local traffic to draw from between you.

1. Coordinate: Choose a morning for everyone to make a post on their Facebook feed at the same time with an advertisement or piece of *content* they want their new traffic to see - think video *content*, a short *animation*, animated logo, or lead magnet although any *content* can certainly do.

2. Participate: Visit the 9 other participants pages and both like their post and leave a good comment.

The best way to do this is offer a statement about what they posted and ask a relevant follow up question that is easy to reply to. Make it good, because they will do the same for yours in turn and the better the prompts, the less time you'll spend trying to generate a conversation with someone who's giving you nothing to work with.

> **Pro tip:** Don't just comment "Great!" or "Really cool stuff, Karen!" Ask a question or otherwise give them a clear path to a response. We need to manufacture a back and forth.

Now each of these 10 posts on these 10 different local businesses suddenly light up with activity and likes and conversations and even though we know what the connections are, Facebook can't quite put it's finger on it. So they just assume what's going on is very popular, people in this city are really excited, and it better help get the word out.

3. Maintain: As you continue to respond to the 9 comments you have on your personal post and all of the organic responses from your own audience, you will have quite the buzz going. Now your post has over 30 comments and growing fast, that's something Facebook will take notice of and it will start putting additional mechanisms into action to expose it to more people from the different connections inside the neural network and that's when things get into action, even if your page is just getting established:

The real advantage to this strategy comes when showing up in *cold traffic* feeds. Your *content* won't be labeled **SPONSORED**, like all the other ads because it's not - it's a popular activity update from a local business they've liked. It will say "*XYZ business* commented on a post by ABC," and people are more likely to investigate activity updates. These "under the radar" Facebook appearances are more effective per exposure than a typical paid ad.

Once one or two people from your audience interact with any of these other businesses and vice versa, it gives Facebook the notion that since these people have this in common, others more likely do too. Then the algorithm will start unlocking cold traffic feeds and showing your activity posts to more and more people on each others lists without paying.

As more likes and comments roll in, those network connections get thicker and stronger; in just a couple cycles you'll be getting new eyeballs from all of the other businesses audiences in your local-link network and more without spending a dime. Add more business pages and add to the reach and there's no limit to how many people can participate but this when done well takes hours every cycle and as business owners who likely don't have the time to do this kind of social media management, it can be incredibly cumbersome to maintain.

The sad truth is that you can probably get the same number of exposures for only $50 in *boosted* ad spend.

A *local-link network* may absolutely be the perfect solution for your business and your city, especially due to the perks, but the system is rigged now so that it's just cheaper and easier for most established businesses to spend the money, boost the post, and be done with it.

The bottom line is simple: although your page earns reach through new connections and activity and engagement which is free, for just a few dollars you can get the same result of hours of work online. Yes, it's a total racket but at the same time it works if you know what you're doing so why resist?

Buying Social Media Advertisements:

The successful social media ad mentality is simple: **"disrupt"** the right person long enough to make your offer and move them to the next step of the sales journey before they get distracted again. That's probably becoming pretty familiar by now, but that's really good because it should be second nature:

"Disrupt, Engage, Collect"

It's actually more important to understand the philosophies and fundamentals behind social media advertising than any combination of advertising strategies or tactics alone. The buttons, options, and tricks may be different a year from now, but understanding how to find the right target, stop a *scroller* in their tracks long enough to absorb your *content* and transition them to your own audience for *retargeting* is a necessity that will be valuable long into the future.

Launching a social media ad has two parts: completing the Audience Targeting section, and adding the advertisement *content* itself.

Both of these have to work together in harmony to earn leads and engagement for your efforts, but be warned there is a learning curve and you shouldn't expect to be wildly successful with your first attempt at running an ad campaign; although I'm 100% rooting for you. You can't get discouraged if it doesn't immediately take off. So get out there and jump in with a few dollars spent.

> *Everybody falls the first time, right, Trin?*
> *(Cypher, The Matrix 1999)*

Social media advertising is a more targeted tool than other traditional advertising platforms like television, radio or print because of how you can find new people based on very specific target criteria. The algorithms in the software will use its vast library of stored personal data to find them with incredible accuracy. If you've targeted or *retargeted* properly and have the right value proposition in place, you're going to see some successes but you might have to try, test, and retry before reaching the sweet spot. That's just part of the ad buying process as a future Marketing Master.

1. Audience "targeting:" If you haven't already explored the Facebook Ad Manager, what you'll find there in the realm of targeting new audiences by specific options and traits should astound you.

Once you know what you want in your ad, getting started couldn't be easier if you've done your target marketing homework and have your *loyals* traits in front of you. Grab your Target Map from Chapter 4 and literally feed these details into the **"audience builder"** when it asks you who you want to find. And if you're looking for cold traffic, it works almost like magic:

- Women. 45-62 years old, divorced and living in

Washington State with household income over $100,000 and likes the brand COACH.
- Anyone with the title, "Business owner," "CEO," or "Entrepreneur," in their position less than a year, with 5 or more employees that follows *Digital Marketer* and serves Business to Consumer markets.
- Homeowners with more than two kids and speak Spanish within 25 miles of zip code 79924.

Targeting isn't a bug of social media like some consumers believ, it's actually a feature. It's a service. It's more effective and it doesn't waste people's time with things that aren't for them.

As a consumer, the thought of so many companies using all this data could be worrisome but as a marketer when you find out how specific you can get with your hunt for new customers you just have to be excited at the possibilities.

Specifically advertising to someone who has engaged with your brand in the past is called **"Retargeting."**

From the *Facebook audience builder* you'll be able to select people from your own audiences based on very unique criteria.

Example: You can retarget with the perfect follow up *ads* specifically to people who:
- *Have liked your page*
- *Have liked something you've posted in the last X months*
- *Have commented on your content*
- *Have watched a particular video on your page*
- *Have watched 50% of a particular video*

- *Have watched any amount of ANY of your videos*
- *Is a man that liked your page*
- *Is a woman that liked your page*
- *Is a member of a group you host*
- *(Plus hundreds of other combinations of actions...)*

...and the *FRIENDS* of anyone who has done these things. Yes, you can target their friends too. That in itself is an overpowered ability because someone who needs what you do will likely know other people who need what you do too and your conversion among these friends is higher than cold traffic. Also, when these people see your *ads*, it will tell them right up front that a friend of theirs has also liked your business and that in itself is a very persuasive social element, but theres much more.

With the right tools connecting your social media accounts to your automation software you can instantly send strategic Facebook ads to people who:

- *Get added to your database*
- *Subscribe to a list*
- *Opted in for content*
- *Opens a certain email*
- *Downloads content*
- *Buys a particular product*
- *Buys any product*
- *Joins your membership*
- *Has a new "opportunity" added*
- *Moves sales pipeline stage*

- *Has a new invoice generated*

And many, many more...

> **Retargeting is one of the most underutilized tools in the modern Marketer's digital arsenal simply because most people don't understand how it works yet.**

As a passionate Automator, retargeting happens to be my favorite part of social media marketing in general:

Imagine meeting the perfect lead at a networking event, adding their contact information to Infusionsoft on your phone app and they immediately start seeing Facebook ads from you loaded with testimonials about why your customers are so glad they chose you.

Imagine sending a campaign email with a special offer and anyone who opens it but doesn't buy is shown Ad's for the offer again and again on Facebook until they act and the Ads automatically stop?

Imagine someone making a purchase and then immediately seeing ads offering them the perfect upsell - all pre-built inside of your automation system and operating largely without you.

Your business can do that - it's not just for huge companies anymore!

Leads don't even know they're being *retargeted*, it just suddenly feels like you're everywhere and that's huge

SOCIAL MEDIA 201: Advertising & Local Link Networks

for building your *authority*.

Your leads are going to be impressed, but more importantly they are going to be a lot more likely to take action as each one of these retarget touches gets them one step closer to the next sales stage, so don't forget to include these incredibly powerful social media *retargeting* functions in your automation blueprint so you can have this system when the time comes.

2. Social Media Advertising Content:

Knowing who to target is as important as knowing what to put in the advertisement itself - if you're to have any hopes of connecting that is. If the targeting is off, your social media ads will end up wasting valuable resources getting in front of people who aren't qualified to do business with you. Even with world class *content*, it just won't be the right fit from the start.

To get the correct ad to the correct person affordably, you're going to have to play ball with Facebook and Instagram's protocol (and others for that matter). Like in all advertising, Marketers have to find ways to navigate around the limitations of each platform while using them to their advantage whenever possible. Begin with the main types of *content* your Facebook and Instagram advertisements can contain:

Text Ads: A solid text advertisement can struggle side by side against a sea of exciting visual content, but that doesn't mean they don't work. There are countless successful text ads running everyday for a reason but you will need good copy with a powerful headline to be disruptive, beyond just having a great offer.

Text posts can be powerful in their simplicity. For the right industries, text based ads are a great option.

Image Ads: Including a visual element is a great way to get someone's attention, but beware, you can post an image with text on it to your business page. If you are going to boost it as an advertisement,

Facebook requires that less than 15% of the image is covered by text. So use images with minimal text as the disruption element and let the burden of the message reside in the *headline and Text Body*.

Image Specifications:

Recommended image size: 1080 × 1080 pixels

Recommended image ratio: 1:1

"**Carousels:**" Multiple images in a single Ad that people can swipe through. The effectiveness of these are contested but they do work best for companies selling physical products. You can share an entire collection or family of products in a single ad where you can get someone looking through it they become very good for brand engagement overall as an interactive experience by nature.

"**Slideshows:**" These collections of photos play automatically as traffic scrolls past and hopes the motion will add an extra element of disruption. Select your photos and set the transition speed or upload videos up to 15 seconds; slideshows are a favorite for promoting experiences and lifestyle brand offers.

"**Video Ads:**" The highest converting *content* in the Social Media Ad world: video and *animation* have natural stopping power and inherently hold audience attention. Video is cheaper to advertise because Facebook knows people like it more and they are in the business of making people happy long enough to market to them; that's very good for those investing in video of any kind.

Facebook Ad Format:

Website Link: You don't just have to put your business website here. This field is where custom domains can completely change how your message is perceived overall. Get creative with a strategic link just for your target ad audience and have that domain *redirect* traffic back to your website or wherever you're sending leads:

www.SurplusDepot.army → *(Redirect to)*
www.SurvivalSupplyDepotSanDiego.com/militarygear

Headline: The Headline is intended to be an advertisement's main idea but it doesn't have to be. Instead of just stating the offer directly, headlines are often strategically positioned to create curiosity, mystery, excitement, outrage or disbelief long enough for someone to investigate the body of your text.

Don't underestimate the power of **"emoticons"** in any ad but particularly in the headline - emoticons are the best secondary visual tool you have for disruption after an image if you're using one.

Text Body: Where the main idea of your value proposition is summarized as persuasively as possible. No matter what kind of advertisement you are running, use the *P.S.P.S. model* to present a journey driving to the Call to Action in the text body along with all the reasons they need to jump on it right then. That way by the time they reach the *C.T.A.* area they know exactly why they should click.

Facebook & Instagram C.T.A. Options:

"**Facebook Ad Manager**," and Facebook Advertising in general will continue to get more intuitive for marketers as it develops. There are now over a dozen different **"Call to Action buttons"** that will help get your audience to take the next step, each with their own advantages, limitations, and special functions. These *Call to Action button* choices are constantly changing, often for the best, but here are some of the basics you absolutely need to be familiar with to run potent Facebook Ads:

- **Learn More**: Sends those who activate to a domain of your choice. An effective, nonthreatening universal C.T.A. option, *Learn More* is very popular for good reason as it's one of the highest consistently converting buttons.
- **Apply Now:** Leads prospects to an application to take the next step. Great for masterminds, programs,

groups, or anywhere exclusivity can be used as a tool.

- **Book Now**: Having an automated web-based calendar lets people schedule your available time right through the button or link in your Facebook ad.
- **Contact Us**: Sends a direct message to your business that notifies you immediately, letting a team member pick up the conversation up inside Facebook Messenger in real time.
- **Donate Now:** The perfect *C.T.A.* for causes and organizations, although there are rules attached to this *C.T.A.* button.
- **Download**: A classic. Download is the perfect button for delivering a targeted *lead magnet* in exchange for valuable contact information.
- **Get Offer**: If you have a coupon or promo code you want to promote, Get Offer is a great choice. This option allows your audience to click and get their discount code sent straight to their email.
- **Get Quote**: Does your business provide something that has a variable price based on the job? *Get Quote* allows for special information to be submitted and alerts your business of the activity.
- **No Button**: Not having a button is a non-threatening way to engage traffic: let the content speak for itself and come off as more genuine. A click on any part of the ad is often as good as a click on a *C.T.A. button* when you've positioned your ad properly.

But be aware that some *C.T.A.* options are limited to certain pages with follower minimums or other thresholds like requiring a minimum number of likes on a page before being able to use all of the functions. This is especially relevant for many new businesses that rely on e-commerce because there is work to be done before they can begin to advertise their products with all of the available tools.

When you know how to effectively pay for exposure and it actually connects with the right people, you will have unlocked the sustainable growth every business owner dreams of, but it will take almost every marketing skill you've learned to this point to find that sweet spot.

HAPPY HUNTING.

CHAPTER 21

THE MEDIA:
Leverage & Controlling the Narrative

"Pay no attention to that man behind the curtain"
(The Wizard of Oz, 1939)

If your business has enough visibility with Major Media, you are going to hit a large portion of your target even if you do a lot of your marketing wrong. You see it every day on every network with companies that have the worst ads in the world. The ones that make you scream at your television and radio. Some are still wildly successful because they are so visible you just can't miss them.

Advertising on the big three Major Media's works on many of the same general principles as digital marketing but with much higher risk and much less reliable data - the big benefit is that they have all of the eyeballs, all of them.

If you want serious attention, you need to set your sights

on these platforms eventually, but not how you may think.

It's important to realize that the larger the ad spend, the larger the potential losses and a miscalculation in the details like target, message, or offer can sink your campaign budget or worse - that's why studying the fundamentals are so important before getting to this point.

Broadcast media marketing includes the traditional platforms with their unmatched reach and visibility. It is true that niche programming has caught up considerably due to their ability to reach specific targets and segments, but it is not as precise as the digital marketing spaces. Social media builds its lists through individual actions taken by an individual person tracked over time. Print, Radio, and Television networks know that a certain type of *content* or programs will likely attract a particular type of person but that's often as far as it goes.

There are many different resources and data sets the networks use to persuade marketers that they're reaching the right amount of the right people, but this data is not always reflected in the results. Your instincts as a marketer will have to partially guide you along the way. I've been lied to by **"Advertising Executives"** in the past so be warned - these people are sales professionals themselves. Whenever dealing with an Ad Exec, remember the golden rule of negotiation: be ready to walk away.

"Print:" Effective both locally and in wider circulation, print has a certain extended *authority* that is both non threatening and authentic. Although it used to only mean newspapers, magazines, trade journals, and other things people held in their hand, like everywhere else the internet has invaded the space in a big way, which is actually a good thing for marketers like us.

Advertising in the Los Angeles Times, The New York Times, The Washington Post, and others, (not to mention your local newspaper) is now more accessible to your business than ever with all of the authority that comes with them. Both major and local publications have become increasingly popular digitally where more accurate metrics can be pulled than old school newspapers alone, putting us back in the digital realm of advertising where things are easier to track and validate.

If you think a publication might have access to the perfect audience for your business, go with your gut. But if you're worried it's too expensive, reach out to their advertising department and inquire about smaller batch target marketing to their digital audience first. There's no harm in asking and it's good to know all of your options, you may even be pleasantly surprised.

Radio: Radio is a very personal medium. It has the power to plug your business into someone's morning drive time or workday routine and for the regular listener, it almost seems to live in their head. Some people listen to audio programming of some kind all day no matter where they are and to those people your message can connect almost subconsciously.

But radio isn't just AM & FM anymore. *Spotify*, *iHeartRadio*, and other digital platforms are big players in the radio space and even though they call themselves "radio," they operate their advertising digitally, making more of the familiar digital rules apply to them than anything else.

Demographics can swing wildly on radio and though that can be troublesome for certain marketers who don't understand their target audience or know how to speak their language, it can be very useful for those who do.

Country stations are going a have a more conservative listener base than the hip hop station and they are older, too - 67% of hip hop radio listeners are 18-34 while 32% of country radio listeners are in the same age group. That's not to be mistaken with the classic hip-hop channel reaching people in their 40s and 50s. NPR penetrates the entire spectrum of political thought, but because listeners are 110% more likely to be C suite executives, there is more advertising for *C.R.M.* and business tools than you'd find in most places. They know the professionals and future professionals are listening. What about new rock? Classic rock? Political talk of both persuasions? Sports? Where do your future top 20% *loyal customers* tune in and when?

If you aren't sure, check it out. Spend a couple days listening to the different channels and programs in your market to see who is advertising where. Many businesses already on certain programing will have been doing so for some time and probably for a reason: it's working. This will give you an idea if it's a good fit and you should always do your research upfront before committing dollars to any network or platform.

Have you ever noticed how many Spanish radio stations there are? That's no accident - Spanish speakers in America are some of the most avid listeners to both AM and FM radio stations. 98% of Hispanics 12 or older tune in each week and listen longer – opening more potential to hear your message.

If you have a product or service that extends beyond language barriers, do what it takes to reach the Hispanic communities if you aren't already.

Es buen negocio

Podcasts: Podcasts are a wonderful platform for advertising because they can be so affordable and reach audiences with better accuracy than *Big Radio*. The podcast market is so **"niched,"** it can be easy to find very specific *content* with a very specific audience base.

Television: If your business serves a wide market or has a universally consumable offer in a space like home goods, automotive, food, physical experiences, fitness, spas or health services of any capacity, you may want to consider television.

You don't have to have the next *Old Spice Guy* Ad to be on TV. Television has come to include local, cable and non-traditional networks like *Hulu* which can be more practical than many marketers realize. There is just so much *content* out there bringing in target audiences.

Did you know that many local television stations will shoot your commercial for free if you buy enough air time on their network? These guys used to be my direct competition out of college as a video marketing company and they're hard to compete with: they have production and distribution wrapped up for one price; that's a hell of an offer. Unfortunately, the local station produced advertisement is not going to be clever or exciting and it's going to look like every other local Ad on TV – bad – but that's fine for most local businesses... It's how they are expected to look. Sometimes they even work better than clever pieces shot by real production crews. It's really about understanding who you are talking to and what they really want to see.

The cost of an ad isn't the only expenditure incurred to get more results as you reach higher **"frequency"** so it may take four or five runs on the evening news before someone picks up the phone or visits, but as soon as you hit that magic number you may have hundreds or thousands of people taking action all at once.

You can't just run one ad and be done, *broadcast media* takes a big budget and nerves of steel.

Traditional Media Ad Pricing:

Buying advertising space on the big three traditional media platforms work on the same principles as the digital platforms you've learned in the sense that more reach will cost more money, but because there is no way to monitor the actual **"impressions,"** prices are a calculation of potential audience pool and variables like time slot. They are largely projections.

These pools are called **"media markets"** and they come in tiers: the more people in an area being reached by the network, the higher the tier, the more expensive the advertising slots are. In a small town or suburb, your ads may be incredibly affordable although running an ad in Los Angeles city Metro, or Dallas, or Chicago, or New York is a very different story.

Sometimes it's best to advertise in smaller markets around a large media market to get the best engagement for the price. Do your research, call your network's advertising department, ask questions and familiarize

THE MEDIA: Leverage & Controlling the Narrative

yourself with the different options so that you can make educated choices. Your business could be making money advertising on TV, on the radio or in print and you don't even realize it.

Being in print, on the radio, and on TV is going to bring in customers, yes, but beyond just that - visibility on these high profile platforms will do amazing things for your authority with people already in your world. It's a total power play for your business no matter how you slice it. So if you're running a campaign with any of these top tier media platforms, integrate it into the rest of your marketing: email it out to your list with how excited you are to see your Ads reaching new lives, post it on your social media - you can even boost your TV, radio, and print media on Facebook and other places so that you can hit people everywhere.

Don't underestimate the added power **"social proof"** has in major media. It's why so many commercials have people being surprised by a product, or people telling a story where they were saved in a situation because of their purchase, even when it's dramatized. If you're not sure what *content* you should go with in your ad, start with this concept of social proof and work it back through the targeting map to make sure you're landing on the right hierarchy of value instead of reconceptualizing the wheel.

Major Media Platforms are expensive and clumsy by nature but the fact is they *HAVE* the traffic. People watch TV, they read print still, and they are listening to more radio than ever - the mediums still perform really well, but I'm going to challenge you to consider another, more accessible option for businesses with smaller marketing budgets:

Pay nothing. It's not quite as precise as buying the traffic outright but using leverage to earn media attention works and it adds a whole other dimension to your business. Consider it a grenade in a fistfight against any competition you might have in the market.

Do you ever see those ads where a multi-billion dollar company runs a commercial about giving a couple thousand dollars or so to a charity? That titan of industry almost certainly spent more on advertising than what they gave. How can they rationalize that? I find it slimy and try not to buy from those companies if it can be helped. I always wonder what other shady things they are up to. It's just not a good look.

The resourceful marketer should do the opposite of what these businesses are doing...

Create an incredible amount of good and then use your marketing skills to get the *Major Media* outlets to cover it. Instead of being the advertiser, be the *content*. It's like tripping the *local link network* and showing up without the "sponsor" designation, people see it and associate you with something positive along with the embedded *C.T.A.*:

> *"People also hire us to XYZ, (← CTA) but today we are excited to be here to talk about (CAUSE)..."*

If they even remotely need "*XYZ*," they will be primed to want to work with you without having to make an offer.

Strength in Action:

What problem is right outside your door? Addiction? Homelessness? Underfunded after school programs? Dirty parks? Potholes? Youth sports team can't make it to regionals?

Maybe they have just been opportunities waiting for you to prove your dedication to the community all along. What if your business became the change it wanted to see in the community, then got the media to notice using your powerful skills of persuasion?

Every local morning program has a place for the human interest piece and there is almost none better than a local business fixing their community one project at a time. They are starved for these stories, so go give them what they want but more importantly, use this opportunity to make a real and lasting change for the people in your area while growing your business. *If that doesn't excite you, forget my book.*

As the Marketer, you have the skills to create your own buzz and leverage to get the *Major Media's* attention. Articles, press releases, Tweets, Facebook LIVE, content videos, social media posts. You can create all of these things to document and build a narrative around your company's mission to make the community a better place while helping your customers with the problem you solve in a big way.

Keep "leaking" this content to the local media networks and eventually someone will bring you on to talk about your work, and once one brings you on the next will be easier, then the next and the next. That's extended local authority that will weave your business into the fabric of your community.

Your good deeds may not get coverage the first time, or the fifth time, but as you continue, the story grows and becomes more worthy of attention while you make more and more of an impact. It may not be enough that you cleaned up the riverside on a Saturday. It may not be enough that you did it ten times. But a point will come where your business will become known as the people who are making a difference and then the community will have to notice; and that always turns into more business in the hands of the resourceful Marketer...

"The Marketer that supports their community will earn their community's support."

CHAPTER 22

COMMENCEMENT

"May the Force be with you" (Star Wars, 1977)

Congratulations! If you've made it through the pages up to this point, then you have earned the right to call yourself a marketer, even if only in theory. Experience is the forge that will temper the skills you've learned here, but now with these new powers, you are both the expert in your field and dangerous at the tactics of sales and marketing; that is a potent combination. Now, with a little resourcefulness you can create success anywhere and grow any business, but most importantly you can now roll up your sleeves and go out to grow yours.

A successful marketer is a strategist, an artist, and a psychologist all at the same time...

That is a great responsibility to wield: the power to influence everyone from those right in front of you to those across the world.

Seeing first hand the darker side of these forces during my time in political marketing scared me; I'm not embarrassed to admit that: It's ugly. It's sloppy. It's exploitative. And it should scare you too. Go out and use these skills and tactics of persuasion, not just to make more money, grow, and gain influence, but I beg you to use these powers for good.

Be a marketer for the people, not against them. Care for your community. Lead with value. Always try to help those precious individuals in your business's orbit be happier and more fulfilled. It's both your privilege and your responsibility.

I've waited until now to make sure you are the right person but at this point you and I have come to a mutual understanding that together we can rise. Just as I learned from the old guard of legendary marketers, today you stand on the shoulders of giants. Anything is possible with diligence and a plan in the hands of the resourceful marketer and their network.

I hope that you use what you have learned to create the master plan and execute it with a clear, singular vision.

Every journey begins with a single step. I don't care if you are from Indiana or India: if you're on a mission to make the world a better place through growing your business then you and I are traveling together.

Support is a funny thing because you never know where you're going to find it. Generations of my family have fought for my privilege of being able to grow a life in the world of business instead of other, more dangerous things. That debt cannot ever be repaid. All I can do now is

COMMENCEMENT

support the do'ers, those who are going to make future generations better and stronger.

If our legacy is a collection of the people we are able to impact during our lifetimes, then I hope you are mine.

As an alumni of The Book on Sales & Marketing, you will get a forever 10% discount on all automation, animation, website building, and support for life. Just register yourself at the link below.

So, go forth and make the future in your image, but if ever you find yourself in a moment of hesitation: remember you and I are now on the same team and Ashley Wilkes is in your corner. Don't wait for support, everything your business needs is at your fingertips...

For help, resources, feedback, and next steps, visit:
TheBookOnSalesAndMarketing.com/Alumni

Alumni Code: AES-2656

VOCABULARY/ APPENDIX:

80/20 Rule (Pareto's Principle): 20% of top efforts yield 80% of total results. (p. 13.)

About Us Page: a page on your website where you share the journey of how your company came to be the leaders in your space or offer the great products that you do. (p. 192.)

Action Button: a clickable button on a site or webpage, action buttons have a short, catchy prompt and should stand out from whatever background they are on. (p. 184.)

Action Color: a color in line with your brand bible that is reserved for calls to action like a button on a page. (p. 168, 184.)

Active Sales: also known as outbound sales, this is the practice of seeking out your leads and contacts for sales conversations whether that be sales calls, emails, texts or otherwise. (p. 141, 147.)

Ad Scent: smell or scent is often the sense attributed to how a piece of marketing feels in relation to the rest of the brand. When a piece of content doesn't smell right to the consumer it can affect their conversion. (p. 170.)

Advertising Executive: an employee of a media network whether that be television, radio or print. Their job is to broker deals with advertisers like you for ad space and can often be negotiated with for better deals, especially if you've built a relationship over time. (p. 220.)

Affiliates: a person or organization who works to make sales on behalf of another. An affiliate is often paid a commission per sale. (p. 62.)

Affiliate Mailing: having an affiliate market your product or service to their audience on your behalf, often for a commission. (p. 31.)

Animation: both an effective and affordable form of video. Animation transcends language and culture, making it potent for offers, and comes with a high level of creative control as opposed to traditional video production which can be subject to limitations from the technical to the circumstantial. (p. 176.)

Audience Builder: A tool inside of the Facebook advertising platform used for selecting specific traits and characteristics of the audience you are trying to reach with your content. (p. 207.)

Authority: the right you have to solve the problem you solve. Both businesses and business owners need to establish and maintain authority. (p. 53, 210, 220.)

Auto-Dialers: software or hardware that automatically makes phone calls to a list, usually handing the conversation off to the salesperson once someone answers. (p.149.)

Automation (i.e. Marketing Automation): the implementation of process and systems to keep up with

Vocabulary/Appendix:

your leads. (p. 71.)

Backlinks: clickable links on one webpage to another that can positively influence the Google ranking of a page. (p. 180.)

Bio Page: a page on your website where you share the personal story of the entrepreneur, owner, or CEO of a company along with a piece of their history and their mission as the leader of the company. (p. 184.)

Bookends: branded animation clips with your logo used at the beginning and end of larger video content to give an added boost of quality (p. 176.)

Boost: Facebook's term for putting advertisement dollars behind that post to get more reach without starting a campaign or doing much else. It will just tell you upfront how many people they will show it to for how much money. (p. 202.)

Booth: a designated space (usually a table) at an event where you can showcase your business to the attendees. Booths can be great opportunities for generating new leads when paired with a relevant lead magnet but be aware, they are rarely free. (p. 22, 130, 194, 196.)

Brand: rules regarding the colors, fonts, vocabulary, and design parameters that your business uses to create digital and physical assets. These rules make it easy for your audience to identify you easily across mediums and helps them recognize you amongst all of the noise. (p. 167.)

Brand Bible: the place where the specific files, details, guidelines for your businesses branding are mapped out and kept for easy access. Everyone on your team who is creating web content, written content, advertising, printing, product development, graphic design, and anything else needs to be in accordance with the brand bible, located in this centralized file or folder. (p. 168, 184.)

Broadcast Marketing: a largely outdated form of marketing where a business blankets an audience with a general message, hoping to hit qualified customers; the epitome of speaking to everyone versus one particular target. Broadcast marketing is highly competitive and therefore notoriously expensive. (p. 18, 77, 127.)

Call Command Center: a secure environment to battle sales anxiety and perform sales calls. (p.146.)

Call to Action (C.T.A.): a place, usually near the end of your email, article, text, video or piece of content where you tell someone exactly what you want them to do and how. (p. 101, 176.)

Call to Action Buttons: a button on a Facebook advertisement that gives you options different options for driving action and engaging your audience. (p. 215.)

Call-Quota: a pre-set number of sales calls that need to be made within a limited period of time. (p. 144, 153.)

Campaign: A coordinated marketing effort to sell a product or service in a defined period. This period is usually a few weeks or months. (p. 74.)

Carousels: a C.T.A. option within Facebook Advertising where multiple images can be displayed in a single Ad that people can swipe through in their timeline. (p. 213.)

Chief Marketer, or *Chief Marketing Officer*: the head

Vocabulary/Appendix:

marketer responsible for spending the budget and setting the action plan for the business. Every successful company must have a chief marketer regardless of how many employees they have. If a business doesn't have a Chief Marketer, the entrepreneur must take on this role. (p. 2.)

Choke Point: the point of contact in which your average lead will decide to purchase the product being offered or not. Whether it be a phone conversation, a face to face sales presentation, or an offer on a landing page; your choke point is where the majority of leads will be presented with the offer and have the opportunity to take action. (p. 42.)

Cold Leads: these prospects usually don't know you from a stranger off the street or have only had a brief interaction with your business. You'll often need to *educate* and *initiate* these leads before they are ready to spend any serious money with you.(p. 43.)

Content: value created for your audience to consume in the form of text, audio, video, and graphic design. Good content will make an impact on in contact's minds with valuable, entertaining and informative pieces. (p. 18, 41, 49-53, 73, 77, 93, 133, 180, 197, 211.)(Chpt. 11, 12, 17.)

Content Marketing: using content to attract an audience to market one's products or services. By providing value in the form of content a business or entrepreneur can establish deep authority allowing all sales to be easier in the future. (p. 50.)

Content Silo: A centralized depository of all the content assets your business owns, the content silo is where you keep all of the content your business is amassing as it grows. Content is useless if you can't find or deploy it and a content silo makes it easy to find what you need easily. (p. 173.)

Conversion Rate: the ratio of contacts that go from one step to the next in any particular part of the sales process, measured in percent. (p. 43.)

Copy: The words used by your business online or offline and can include advertisements, sales emails, video scripts, webpages and anything your business uses to reach its audience. (p. 99.)

Core-Offer: also known as a primary offer, the core offer you want your customers to take and its the product you want your business to be known for. You may have The core offer is central to how the company is perceived. (p. 85-86.)

C.R.M. Customer Relationship Management: The process by which one becomes aware of a prospect, converts them into a lead, sells them a product and then assists with after sale offers and support. The important thing about C.R.M. is that it is much cheaper to maintain an existing relationship with a customer than to get a new customer. (p. 27, 137.)

C.S.V. (Comma Separated Value): a standardized file type that's easily shared between all of the major Customer Relationship Management systems or *C.R.M.s* and the other tools that become necessary as your business grows. (p. 28.)

Database: the marketers database can also be known more informally as your list. This centralized collection of data is where you keep all of your leads, customers, partners,

Vocabulary/Appendix:

and affiliates personal and business contact information for tracking, marketing, and easy access. (p. 26.)

Database Management: a necessary job that needs to be performed to get the most out of the information stored in the database. Database management includes things like deleting duplicate contact entries, cleaning up segmentation, and running relevant reports on a regular basis to maintain the health of the list. (p. 157.)

Data Fields: individual types or pieces of information, a database is made up of data fields such as name, email, phone number, occupation, age, gender, or anything else you choose to record. (p. 26.)

Deep-Dive: an extended session that goes in depth on a particular subject of importance. Often found at the beginning of a new project, the deep dive is used by professionals and experts to find out how to best serve their client. (p. 18.)

Delicious Offer: an offer positioned perfectly with the right value in front of a qualified target. When planned strategically, a delicious offer is hard for audiences to resist. (p. 116)

Deliverability: is the ability of your marketing emails to make it past the *SPAM* and promotions folders into your recipients actual *inbox* (p. 133.)

Digital Legitimacy Test: Proving to prospects and leads that your business is who you say it is. New contacts will often spend no more than 30-45 seconds looking you up on Google and social media before making a decision about taking a next step with your business. (p. 49.)

Digital Manual Labor: The marketers equivalent to picking weeds, digital manual labor includes but is not limited to sending standardized welcome emails, reminders, follow ups, invoices, responding to social media posts, and all of the other things that are important to your success but are time consuming, tedious, repetitive, and take you away from the more unique work you could be doing. (p. 156.)

Disruption: purposefully interrupting someone's behavior long enough for them to absorb your message. (p. 194, 206, 213.)

Docu-Content: content generated by documenting your business in the act of doing what it does best and is in contrast to expensive professional content creation. Docu-content is one of the more effective and affordable strategies for establishing authority. (p. 50.)

Domain: the "home address" of a website, a domain is the location you will find specific pages, often beginning with a "www." and ends with a domain extension such as ".com" or ".org." (p. 189.)

Double Opt-In: by formally confirming your connection through a double opt-in process your recipient is giving you a golden ticket straight into their inbox after which none of your emails will ever get sent to their promotions or SPAM folder from then on. (p. 134.)

E-Commerce: deployment of a digital store where people can buy products or services unassisted. (p. 191.)

Education: a critical stage of the welcoming process for new contacts, education includes teaching your audience more about what you do and why it's important for them

Vocabulary/Appendix:

to choose you over anyone else in the market. (p. 43, 73.)

Efficiency: the science of reducing waste and improving quality. Efficiency comes from the rigorous implementation of systems and processes. (p. 155.)

Email Body: key organ in the anatomy of an email, the email body is where you do the majority of your communicating. Use this area to convey points and benefits to the reader engaging with your call to action which should be found in every marketing email. (p. 131.)

Email Marketing: using the medium of email to nurture contacts and stay top of mind so that you can make a sale when they are ready to buy, (p. 127.)

Engagement: this efficiency metric is used when the lead performs a desired action and can include but is not limited to liking, sharing, or commenting on social media, opening an email, clicking an offer as well as making purchases. (p. 42, 74, 114.)

Facebook Ad Manager: a set of tools and dashboards inside the larger Facebook platform that allows you to manage different aspects of your Facebook advertising from content, audiences, and C.T.A. options. (p. 215.)

Facebook LIVE: an incredibly disruptive type of content, Facebook Live plays a video you are recording in real time inside of your audiences Facebook Feed without the delay of editing or uploading. Simply speak into the camera and people will be able to like, comment, and react to you as you are recording. (p. 52.)

Forecasting: like a weatherperson, a Chief Marketer must be able to estimate how successful a marketing strategy will be before an investment is made. (p. 80.)

Frequency: the number of times your target is exposed to an ad or offer. (p. 224.)

"From" field: found in the anatomy of an email, this field precedes the subject line can plays a huge determining in whether your email will be opened (p. 130.)

Funnel: an escalating series of offers designed to take an opportunity through the sales process maximizing its engagement along the way (p. 2.)

    Lead Magnet → Trip Wire → Core Offer → Upsell

Ghost Text: by adjusting the text at the beginning of an email we can influence it to present a different message in the preview window than what is actually in the email itself. (p. 131.)

Google Index: the priority in which Google chooses to display one website or piece of content over another. (p. 188.)

Greeting Zone: an area of the email that can be previewed inside email management software that lets the recipient read the first sentence or two so they can decide whether or not to open. (p. 131.)

Hex Code: the standardized color sharing format that allows creatives to make sure they are getting the correct shade and hue of the color they are looking for. (p. 169.)

High Touch Conversational Marketing (H.T.C.M.): this is a technique to fill for the shortcomings of conventional marketing by inspiring more direct interaction with customers. Live chat is an example of this. Done well it

Vocabulary/Appendix:

makes the customer feel highly valued and more likely to continue buying from that company. (p. 77.)

Home Page: the brain of your website, the home page gives visitors a general overview of who you are and what to expect from your business. (p. 182.)

Hot Leads: these people already know, love, and trust you. These are your customers, *loyals*, and anyone who has made significant purchases with you in the last 180 days. (p. 44.)

Impressions: an advertising metric used to define anytime someone is exposed to an ad or boosted post. (p. 224.)

Inbox: where your contacts receive their wanted emails. Not to be confused with the SPAM or promotions folders which are to be avoided.(p. 133.)

Initiation: an integral part of the welcoming of new contacts. Show them what to expect in terms of value how to interact with your brand. This is where you introduce value early on, in part to get them in the habit of checking your desired method of communication whether that be email, blog, social media, a membership site or otherwise. (p.73.)

Intro-preneur: a new entrepreneur. Someone learning the ropes. (p. 49.)

Journey: more than just the product or service, your audience wants to buy how you came to be here and the mission you are on. If you can sell them on your journey you will earn a loyal customer. (p. 6.)

Knock: a direct attempt to reach a prospect on the phone or in person with the intention of making them a direct offer. (p. 144.)

Landing Page: A webpage that prospects "land on" that is designed to get information from a prospect, such as email address, name and/or phone number and is for one purpose only. Unlike a website, the viewer only has two options, submit or close the page manually. Landing pages are great for special offers, lead generation, and lots of places where something might only be available for a limited time. (p. 187.)

Lavaliere: an affordable microphone that's easy to use and can be discreetly attached to the talent without impeding their motion or sacrificing great audio. (p. 174.)

Lead Magnet: something valuable that a prospect will trade their contact information to acquire. Lead magnets are infinitely varied but must always be reflect the value proposition you'll be presenting in the core offer. (p. 81.)

List: (see database)

Loaded Question: a question used in the sales conversation that positions you for a favorable response regardless of their answer. (p. 195.)

Local Link Network: a fabricated network of connections between Facebook business pages used to unlock more reach for its participants without paying for it. (p. 202.)

Logo: the signature art you use to represent your business. Having a logo is not the same as having a brand. (p. 7, 170.)

Long Form Sales Format: most commonly found

Vocabulary/Appendix:

on landing pages and in sales emails, long form sales formats were very effective in the past but are no longer as consistent as they used to be (p. 132.)

Love Letter: an alternative to newsletter, love letters are curated content sent to prospects based on their segmentation. A love letter got its name because people will love to get them. (p. 136.)

Loyal (loyal customer): in your top 20% of revenue generators. They come back and spend more, more often. (p. 13.)

Major Media: the traditional media platforms, television, radio, print. (p. 22.)

Media Markets: tiers used to regulate the pricing of advertising, media markets are determined by the amount of total potential viewers in an area that will be exposed. (p. 224.)

Merged Fields: codes within a software platform that can be injected into automated content to display customized information to the reader, often from your database or other fluid pieces of information. They can be used to replace names, dates, lead sources, upcoming events and more to make email from a system feel more unique. (p. 159.)

Meta Data: information hidden within the back end of a website that Google uses to determine relevance and priority for its users. Meta data will impact your Google Ranking when people search for words related to your industry. (p. 186.)

Newsletter: newsletters are composites of relevant

information and are intended to keep you top of mind with your audience. (p. 135.)

Niche: a specific group within the larger audience that you may be able to serve. A niche is a percentage of the larger group that possesses specific traits that a business may find more desirable than regular customers off the street. (p. 223.)

Noise: the barrage of stimulus your target experiences on a daily basis that interferes with them hearing your message. (p.13, 18, 96.)

Nurture: the building of a relationship with your *target* over time by providing value until they are ready to make a purchase. (p. 14, 73, 128.)

Objection: an excuse a prospect gives for not buying when presented with an *offer*. (p. 44, 147, 151.)

Offer: more than just a product or a service, an offer is positioned at a special price for a specific reason that will increase perceived value of the purchase to the buyer. (p. 13, 27, 40, 79, 85, 99, 113, 147, 182, 194.) (Chpt. 13.)

Offer frequency: the average amount of times that a qualified prospect must be exposed to an offer before they take action. (p. 79.)

Opportunity: a lead, prospect, or current customer you've qualified for a new purchase. (p. 72, 210, 221.)

Opt-in: how contacts give you permission to email them. This alone won't always mean that they will get everything you send as Google and the other email providers are becoming increasingly diligent. To really defeat the *SPAM*

Vocabulary/Appendix:

and *promotions folders* deploy a *double opt-in* process. (p.128, 131.)

Organic: reach or exposure earned without being paid for. (p. 202.)

Pain Point: the unhappiness someone experiences as a result of not having your product or service; feeling cramped in their current home, not having the perfect outfit for a big day, or feeling neglected by their current service provider. Addressing pain points directly in the sales cycle helps qualified targets visualize how much happier they will be after they make their purchase. "Pain points are paying points." (p. 82, 97.)

Pareto's Principle: (see 80/20 rule)

.PDF: a portable document format, .PDFs are the are the easiest and most common way of sharing professional documents. (p. 81.)

Pop Up: a window that interrupts a visitors interaction with a website to give them the opportunity to act. (p. 184.)

Power hour: also known as a "Pareto-hour," the power-hour is 60 minutes dedicated to completing or working on a single task without distraction or interruption and can be used to manufacture more of the top 20% of actions that yield 80% of your results. (p. 59.)

P.S. (Post-Script): an important part of email anatomy. The P.S. is heavily trafficked by those who open your email while they scroll to the bottom to see how long it is before reading. Your P.S. should always either restate the main C.T.A. of the email or present another option for those the first may not have been right for. (p. 132.)

P.S.P.S (Problem Solution Problem Solution) model: a content creation model wherein one solves problems for leads in steps that builds authority as it goes. It eliminates objections and leads to a quicker sale. (p. 104.)

Preview Window: email anatomy – what can be viewed by a lead before they open the email. The preview window content needs to be compelling enough to get them to open the email. (p. 130.)

Primary C.T.A.: the main *call to action* in a message or piece of content. You may have multiple opportunities for the consumer to take action, but there should always be one main thing you want the majority of them to do. That's its Primary C.T.A. (p. 132.)

Primary Offer: (See core offer)

Print: newspapers, magazines, and community publications that are still very popular with many audiences. (p. 220.)

Production Value: the overall quality of a video or animation. (p. 176.)

Promise of the Premise: originally a filmmaking term that works very well in marketing, the promise of the premise is a social contract between the customer and the business that they will receive what they were promised. (p. 106.)

Quick-pitch: a condensed, more potent version of your larger pitch. Sometimes referred to as the "elevator pitch" with the idea that you have a time equivalent of the distance between two floors on an elevator to sell a prospect on your idea. (p. 42.)

Redirect: sending digital traffic from one page to another

Vocabulary/Appendix:

either with or without their knowledge. (p. 180, 186.)

Retarget: paying for advertisement that will be shown to someone who has already encountered your business somehow. Using the Facebook advertising options, you can create a list to retarget based on anyone who has taken even small actions in the past. Retargeting can make it feel like your business is everywhere and can greatly improve authority in a short period of time. (p. 206, 208.)

R.O.I. (Return on Investment): the measure of resources generated versus resources expended, whether those be time, money, influence, or manpower. (p.13.)

Revenue Threshold: a number of revenue dollars that once spent will designate a customer as a VIP. (p. 117.)

Robo Calls: automated dialing machines that will call a list and deliver a prerecorded message. (p.149.)

Rot: opportunities will expire if you wait too long (p. 114.)

Sales Call Anxiety: a challenge some salespeople experience before and during sales calls, often caused by worrying they are going to be judged for saying the wrong thing. (p. 144)

Sales choke: see Chokepoint. (p.42.)

Sales cycle: all the components and steps that lead to a sale, from prospect to finished transaction.(p. 15, 43, 65.)

Sales Packing: bundling additional products at the point of sale. (p. 89.)

Sales Pipeline: a series of steps to take your leads down to get them to buy. Not the same thing as a funnel, a pipeline can aid your sales process. (p. 41, 73, 153.)

Sales Process: the steps you take your lead through from where they are now, to where they purchase. Sales processes don't have to be long, they just have to be appropriate for your audience and the product you are selling. (p. 41.)

Sales Session: a dedicated time to make active sales efforts. (p. 152.)

Sales stage: the components of the sales cycle. They are: Lead Generation; Qualify Leads; Demonstrate Value; Product Knowledge; Sales and Support. (p. 26.)

Salesy: the feeling or vibe a person gives off when they are being disingenuous. (p. 68, 80.)

Salutation: email anatomy - how you sign off of your emails. Sincerely, best, love, a consistent salutation helps with establishing tone with your readers over time. (p. 132.)

Scroll or "Scrolling:" looking through a timeline on social media with little other particular purpose but finding something interesting or new. (p. 49.)

Search Engine Optimization (SEO): organizing information on your website so that Google finds it more valuable and will rank it higher in searches. (p. 180.)

Segmentation: separating a larger list into smaller groups by type or behavior for easier and more intimate follow up. (p. 32.)

Self Selection: the phenomenon where a message resonates so strongly with someone that they seek you out to help

Vocabulary/Appendix:

them instead of the other way around. (p. 97.)

Shotgun Mic: a microphone that is held near the subject but often out of sight. Shotgun mics are connected to a recorder and pointed at the subject rather than attached like a lavaliere. (p. 174.)

Signature: part of the anatomy of an email, the signature comes after the salutation but above the postscript and it's where you list your name and any other relevant information like position or credentials. Your signature can be used to establish authority or create familiarity if positioned correctly. (p. 132.)

Simple Sales Formula:

Offer + Lead + Sales Process = Revenue (p. 39.)

Skin: a tool used to change the look of something without changing the structure or overall format. Skins are a great way to keep websites and other softwares looking fresh without starting from scratch. (p. 181.)

Slideshow: a Facebook advertising option for making images more disruptive. (p. 219.)

SMS Text Messages: a great way to make sure that your audience sees your message. (p. 147.)

Social Proof: in the form of testimonials, reviews, and endorsements. People want to see that what you do has worked for other people. Social proof motivates cold traffic to act more than almost any other single type of content. (p. 225.)

Solo-preneur: An entrepreneur who does not have a team working with them. (p. 1.)

SPAM: unwanted emails with no value, often (p. 128, 132.)

Speak-to-Sell: using public speaking to sell your business by using authority to grow your authority, list, and exposure to larger audiences. (p. 197)

Speaking their *(your customers)* **Language:** using the same words, terms, and phrases that your customers use when talking about what you do and their related pain points.(p. 93.)

Spreadsheet: a field of cells where you can enter data. For free spreadsheet access visit. (p. 28.)

Social Media Integration: sharing one post or piece of content on several social media platforms to reduce the need to create more original content quickly. (p. 55.)

Social Media Management: upkeep of a businesses social media presence online, including posting new content, engaging with comments and visitors, addressing complaints, and the general appearance of brand to the public. (p. 57.)

Social Media Marketing: tapping into the traffic social media generates for promoting your business. Your social media marketing should give people a deeper relationship with you. (p. 48.)

Sponsorship: paying an organizer for access to an event in return for exposure to their audience. Can come in many forms including presentation in their media, an introduction, or even the opportunity to address their group. (p. 193, 204.)

Vocabulary/Appendix:

Stinger: a short audio cue used in videos to give them higher production value and brand alignment. (p. 175.)

Subject Line: email anatomy: the subject line is seen before your email is even opened and is the second thing most recipients will notice after who the email is from. Your subject line must be compelling enough to persuade them to open it. The most influential part of your emails overall success or failure. (p. 130.)

Swag: free branded merchandise one can use to generate leads or increase brand awareness and influence their perception of the brand. (p. 195.)

Tag: a tool for segmenting a list by things like behavior, category, or sales stage. Tags are used to distinguish between contacts and will allow you to send particular messages to the right groups without sending it to everyone or doing it manually. (p. 32, 158.)

Talking Head Video: videos where the subject is delivering a message directly into the camera, talking straight to th viewer. Talking head videos can be effective but feel flat or boring so be conscious of ways you can improve production value such as choosing a dynamic background, adding your logo, and using bookends. (p. 176.)

Target Customer: also known as an ideal customer, your target is a specific audience with traits that make them great prospects for becoming loyal customers. (p. 18.)

Target Map: a document containing the specific traits, characteristics, attributes, known locations, and personality notes that you will rely on as you plan your target marketing. (p. 20.)

Target Marketing: the action of marketing to a desired market segment. By mapping exactly who a business is looking to attract, it becomes much easier to locate them in their natural daily activities. The more effectively targeted marketing is, the cheaper it is to execute. (p. 15.)

Targeting: the hunt for your preferred target. (p. 207.)

Task: an item on an agenda that needs to be done by a person. A task is one step in a multi-step sales pipeline to accomplish an objective. (p. 159.)

Telemarketer: a person whose sole job is to make outgoing sales calls and deliver a script. Known for interrupting dinner. (p. 143.)

Testimonial: a review of your business that you can use in your marketing as social proof that what you do works. The most influential content on your website for future buyers. (p. 183.)

Thank You Page: a page that is displayed after a visitor takes action or submits their information on a website or landing page. A thank you page traditionally confirms whatever the contact just did but can be positioned tactically to take them to the next step in the sales process. (p. 186.)

Tone: is what the message "sounds like". The tone is how the intended audience interprets a message. Different targets need a different tones. (p. 101, 175.)

Top of Mind (T.O.M.): a monique for nurturing a prospect. By regularly reaching out to someone with

Vocabulary/Appendix:

valuable information or content you will stay on the top of their mind, making them go straight to you instead of your competitors when it's time to buy. (p. 134.)

Touch: a point of contact in the sales process whether that be a phone call, SMS text, opened email, consumed content, advertising exposure, or any other way someone is reminded of the value your business provides. (p. 75.)

Traffic: an active audience that can be used for your marketing. (p. 22.)

Trip Wire: often between $3 - $9, a trip wire is an aggressively priced offer that tempt leads to get out their wallet. This is because a psychological change happens when a lead becomes a customer. Anyone who gives you some money is 2000% more likely to spend more money with you. (p. 84.)

Upsell: an offer that exploits the psychological concept of value in such a way as to justify spending more money. The classic example is the cinema, where the small popcorn is $6.99 but the medium (twice as much popcorn) is "only" $7.99. Thus, almost no one buys the small and get at least the medium (or possibly the large; it's only another dollar more). (p. 88.)

Upsell Protocol: rules a business implements to maximize their spend per transaction. Every product should have an adjoining upsell to be offered every time somebody purchases that item. (p. 89.)

Value Ladder: the factor in your business that your customers find valuable listed in order from top to bottom.

(p. 35.)

V.I.P.: a designation your business can give for any contact to get them to act. Anyone can be a V.I.P. for any reason you decide from returning customer, to first time shoppers. V.I.P. incentives can encourage customers to take further action by exploiting their desire for exclusivity. (p. 117.)

Video Ads: paid exposure for a video to promote your business. Video ads get extended reach due to inherent entertainment value video holds. Video ads are cheaper to run and more engaging than text or image ads. (p. 213.)

Video Batching: recording multiple videos in one filming session. Video batching reduces the cost per video by creating more videos at a time. Bring additional changes of clothes and have copy prepared to make the most of video shoot investments. (p. 172.)

Video Script: copy written beforehand so that the filming process is smoother and the finished result more impactful. (p. 175.)

Voicemail: leaving a message for a lead after a sales call. Can lead to mixed results based on your performance. (p. 149.)

Voice-over: using the voice of a performer played over a video to communicate more or give context to the visuals. (p. 175.)

Warm Leads: those people who already know and like you. Warm leads are more likely to buy with just a gentle reminder of the value you provide. (p. 43.)

Whale: the top 20% of your *loyal customers*. Whales buy more, more often. (p. 13, 44.)

Whiteboard Video: a stylized type of animated video that replicates the look of drawings on a whiteboard, often with a visible hand drawing your images on the screen. (p. 177.)

Writers Room: a safe space with qualified individuals to discuss creative projects. (p. 102.)

WordPress: completely customizable. WordPress is the most versatile and powerful website building platform. WordPress is used by all of the best and biggest brands and is superior to all other builder platforms in every way but one. WordPress can be difficult for new users without a technology or coding background but because WordPress and Google work perfectly in tandem, an optimized site on WordPress is the most powerful business tool on the internet. (p. 180.)

Working Leads: implementing a sales quota, strategically following a process to reach opportunities, and documenting the results. Working leads is a critical part of any businesses success. (p. 147.)

There is much more information, examples, and support waiting for you at:

www.TheBookOnSalesAndMarketing.com/Mastery

THE BOOK ON SALES AND MARKETING

Notes:

Notes:

Notes:

Notes:

Made in the USA
Las Vegas, NV
18 July 2022